CAMBRIDGE LIBRARY COLLECTION

Books of enduring scholarly value

History

The books reissued in this series include accounts of historical events and movements by eye-witnesses and contemporaries, as well as landmark studies that assembled significant source materials or developed new historiographical methods. The series includes work in social, political and military history on a wide range of periods and regions, giving modern scholars ready access to influential publications of the past.

The Abbot's House at Westminster

In this 1911 work, J. Armitage Robinson uses architectural and documentary sources to discuss the history of the abbot's buildings at Westminster Abbey. The medieval monastic remains are extensive, but have been considerably modified over the centuries. The abbey muniments provide much information on the building's history, and Robinson includes many documents, both medieval and post-Reformation, to trace the development of the complex and how it was used. As dean of the abbey, Robinson had unprecedented access, and so was able to work out the architectural history more fully than had been possible in previous studies. As the abbey grew in importance and wealth, so the status of the abbot grew, necessitating grander buildings for entertaining. The medieval abbey must have been a continual building site, to judge by the frequent references to structural work in the accounts. This is a valuable study of an important surviving medieval building.

Cambridge University Press has long been a pioneer in the reissuing of out-of-print titles from its own backlist, producing digital reprints of books that are still sought after by scholars and students but could not be reprinted economically using traditional technology. The Cambridge Library Collection extends this activity to a wider range of books which are still of importance to researchers and professionals, either for the source material they contain, or as landmarks in the history of their academic discipline.

Drawing from the world-renowned collections in the Cambridge University Library, and guided by the advice of experts in each subject area, Cambridge University Press is using state-of-the-art scanning machines in its own Printing House to capture the content of each book selected for inclusion. The files are processed to give a consistently clear, crisp image, and the books finished to the high quality standard for which the Press is recognised around the world. The latest print-on-demand technology ensures that the books will remain available indefinitely, and that orders for single or multiple copies can quickly be supplied.

The Cambridge Library Collection will bring back to life books of enduring scholarly value (including out-of-copyright works originally issued by other publishers) across a wide range of disciplines in the humanities and social sciences and in science and technology.

The Abbot's House at Westminster

J. Armitage Robinson

CAMBRIDGE UNIVERSITY PRESS

Cambridge, New York, Melbourne, Madrid, Cape Town, Singapore,
São Paolo, Delhi, Dubai, Tokyo, Mexico City

Published in the United States of America by Cambridge University Press, New York

www.cambridge.org
Information on this title: www.cambridge.org/9781108013604

This edition first published 1911
This digitally printed version 2010

ISBN 978-1-108-01360-4 Paperback

NOTES AND DOCUMENTS

RELATING TO

WESTMINSTER ABBEY

No. 4

THE ABBOT'S HOUSE AT WESTMINSTER

CAMBRIDGE UNIVERSITY PRESS
London: FETTER LANE, E.C.
C. F. CLAY, Manager

Edinburgh: 100, PRINCES STREET
Berlin: A. ASHER AND CO.
Leipzig: F. A. BROCKHAUS
New York: G. P. PUTNAM'S SONS
Bombay and Calcutta: MACMILLAN AND Co., Ltd.

THE ABBOT'S HOUSE AT WESTMINSTER

BY

J. ARMITAGE ROBINSON, D.D.

DEAN OF WELLS

Cambridge :
at the University Press
1911

Cambridge:
PRINTED BY JOHN CLAY, M.A.
AT THE UNIVERSITY PRESS

PREFACE

NO English monastery has retained so much of its ancient buildings intact as the Abbey of Westminster. When the monks were forced to depart, the Refectory and the Infirmary Chapel were stripped of their lead and became dangerous ruins which were soon cleared away: the Convent Kitchen and the Misericorde survived only a little longer. But almost everything else lent itself with slight modification to practical uses. The Chapter House became a magazine of State records: the Dormitory was divided between a Library and a Schoolroom. And the prebendaries made themselves houses with, at first, but little structural alteration of the various halls and chambers of the old monastic officers. The Granary, the Gatehouse and the Almonry were very slow to disappear: prints and plans of the eighteenth century have preserved to us their main features. A modern crust has formed over very much of the medieval work, partly destructive indeed, but partly also protective.

If the monastery had survived to witness a great movement of reform like that of the Maurists in France, far more would have been lost to the antiquary of our days, who may be truly thankful that the crash came as soon as it did. There would be more work to admire of the style of the Little Cloisters and the present Dormitory of the King's Scholars; but much that is of surpassing beauty, and almost everything that is of historical interest outside the church itself, would have been carefully reformed away.

It is a matter of surprise that so little has been done to map out and describe with exactness the remains of the monastic buildings. The late Mr Micklethwaite first brought to bear upon the question the necessary combination of architectural and antiquarian knowledge. His valuable *Notes on the monastic buildings at Westminster* must be the basis of any future investigations. But he laboured under two great disadvantages. His work was done long before he was made surveyor of the fabric, and there were many domestic interiors to which he had no access. Moreover the resources of the Muniment Room were not at his disposal: he was not himself qualified for their investigation, even if the arrangement of the documents had gone far enough to make such researches possible. The present short study will incidentally offer some help to those who will concern themselves in the future with the topography of the Abbey. I have indeed found it necessary to the particular topic with which I deal to make a courageous attempt at a plan of those portions of the buildings which adjoin the Abbot's House. This plan must be taken as the work of an amateur, who has had to combine parts of old and new plans of varying scales and of unequal degrees of exactitude. It will be discarded, of course, when new workers carry forward the enquiry; but meanwhile it may serve to correct some mistakes of the past, as well as to illustrate some of the documents which are here printed.

The Abbot's House has escaped the ravages of time and restoration better than any other part of the domestic buildings of the monastery. The change which it has undergone has been almost entirely of the nature of addition. The additions themselves are worth studying, and the more so because to a large extent they can be exactly dated. Accordingly, while my main interest has been in the medieval portions, I have added a series of documents which throw light upon the later history. I cannot guarantee the exactness of the transcripts of some of these later documents in minute particulars. I have taken them from my notebooks, and have not been able to verify them. But they will serve their purpose as a guide to the material which still awaits systematic treatment. For the medieval period I take full responsibility, for my work upon it was practically completed while it was still my privilege to live in the Abbot's House.

I have to thank my friends Mr Wallace, the Assistant Surveyor of the Abbey, and Mr Gladwyn Turbutt for kind assistance of a technical character. I have not added an Index; for it seemed that reference would be better facilitated by a full Table of Contents.

THE DEANERY, WELLS.

Translation of St Edward, 1911.

CONTENTS

PAGE

PREFACE v

I. THE ABBOT'S CAMERA IN THE NORMAN MONASTERY 1
The Turret Staircase 5
An earlier building on the site of Jerusalem Chamber . . . 7

II. THE WORK OF ABBOT LITLYNGTON 9

III. SUBSEQUENT DEVELOPMENTS 13

IV. ILLUSTRATIVE DOCUMENTS AND NOTES 16

A. Flete's Description of Litlyngton's Building Operations . . 16

B. Summaries and Specimens from Litlyngton's Accounts . . 16
1. Summary of Payments for the Abbot's House . . . 16
2. Extracts relating to Litlyngton's building operations . 17

C. The Six Oaks requested for the Abbot by the King . . . 20

D. The Story of the Lead lent to the Abbot 21

E. The Lease to the Widowed Queen 22

F. The Grant to Bishop Thirlby 24
Cheynygates—Cawagium—Blackestole—Oxehall . . . 26
The King's Almshouse—Bakehouse and Brewhouse . . 27

G. Dissolution Inventories 30
The Butterye 30
The Mysericorde 34
The Kechyn wythin Cheyngate 35
Mr Thyxtyls Chamber—Mr Meltons Chamber—Sulyards chamber—Mr Morres Chamber—The gallorye—Jerusalem parlor 37
The entrie—Jerico parlor—My lordys newe Chappell—the lyttle Chamber nexte—The Halle. 38
The Skolyons Chamber—The Portors lodge—Syr Radulphis Chamber—the lyttle chamber over the comon Jakys—Adames Chamber—Tytleys Chamber—Gabriels chamber—Wardrobe at Cheneygates 39
The Stable—Fullers Chamber—Nuttingis Chamber—Busbyes Chamber—Patchys Chamber 41

PAGE

The Priors House 41
The masshyng house—Thomelis chamber—Saynt Johns House —the mylhouse—the goddis blessing house—the Ealing house—the bake House 43
The Covent Kychen—the salt howse—the blake parlor—the Wetlarder 45
The Farmari—Seynt Kateryns Chappell 46

H. The Dean's House in the Bishop's time 50
The site of the Prior's House—Leases 50

I. The Site of the Misericorde 54

J. Notices relating to the Deanery 58
1—4. Under Dean Bill and Dean Goodman 58
5—10. Dean Neile's *Memoriall.* Accounts and Inventories 59
11—13. Dean Williams 64
14—21. Bradshaw's Chamber—Erections on the S.W. Tower . 65
John Bradshaw's contention with the Governors—His Lease 66
Items of his Bills 73
22. Dean Sprat 75
23, 24. Dean Atterbury—Plans made for his alterations . 76
25. Dean Wilcocks 78

K. The Norman Chequer Work 81

L. Where was the Abbot's Chapel 83

ILLUSTRATIONS

Plan of 'Abbots Roome' and 'Landry' (from Plan of 1715) . . . . *p.* 6
Plan of part of First Floor of the Deanery . . *between pp.* 6 *and* 7
The Norman Chequer Work . . . . *to face p.* 82
Portion of Plan of 1690 . . . . *to face p.* 82
Sketch Plan of part of the Monastic Buildings . . . *in pocket of cover*

* This map is available as download from www.cambridge.org/9781108013604

THE ABBOT'S HOUSE.

I. THE ABBOT'S CAMERA IN THE NORMAN MONASTERY.

The cloister of Westminster, in accordance with the normal Benedictine plan, lay on the south side of the church, the nave of which formed its northern boundary. The east walk was bounded by the south transept, the chapter-house and part of the dormitory; the south walk by the refectory, and the west walk by the cellarer's offices.

The last-mentioned point in this arrangement was varied at a later period: but it accords with the Norman-French poem on the Life of St Edward, written in the middle of the thirteenth century, which thus describes the cloister and its surrounding buildings[1]:

> Clostre i fait, chapitre a frund,
> Vers Orient vouse e rund;
> U si ordené ministre
> Teingnent lur secrei chapitre;
> Refaitur e le dortur
> E les officines entur.
>
> A cloister there he made, chapter-house in front
> Towards the east vaulted and round;
> Where his ordained ministers
> Might hold their secret chapter;
> Frater and dorter
> And offices round about.

More definite evidence of the position of the cellarer's offices is afforded by the Customary of Abbot Richard de Ware which belongs to the latter half of the same century. Here we find the rule that 'while the convent is sitting in chapter no brother, as also no secular, shall pass across outside before the door of the chapter-house on that

[1] *Lives of Edward the Confessor* (ed. Luard), Rolls Series, p. 90.

side of the cloister, nor on the other side over opposite next the cellarer's offices (*juxta celarium*), unless bidden to do so[1].'

The author of the poem quoted above assigns the completion of the monastic buildings to St Edward: but we have good proof that the cloister (and perhaps the refectory also) was built under Abbot Gilbert in the reign of William Rufus. In 1807 a sculptured stone was found in a partition wall between the Mitre and Horn Taverns in Union Street. This wall was the remnant of a Gate on the west side of the Palace Court, called the High Tower, begun by King Richard III in 1484, but left unfinished, and at length demolished in 1706. This stone is figured in Brayley and Britton's *History of the Ancient Palace of Westminster*[2]. There can be little doubt that it formed the capital of one of the pillars of the Norman cloister. Three sides of it are sculptured, each side presenting a group of three figures: (1) the abbot with a pastoral staff, a monk behind holding a closed book, and another in front holding an open book with the words EGO SVM; (2) three men, of whom the one in the centre holds a long open roll; (3) a seated figure holding an open scroll with his two hands, probably the king, with the abbot on his right and a monk on his left. The following portions of inscriptions above the groups remain:

(1) ...CLAVSTRVM · ET · REL?E?...
(2) ...V · SVB · ABBATE · GISLE...
(3) ...· WILLELMO · SECVN....

As the wall of the refectory which bounds the south walk of the cloister retains on its southern face remains of Norman arcading, we may not unreasonably suppose that the four letters of the inscription, which look like REL followed by a broken E, represent the first part of the word REFECTORIVM. This great hall, 170 ft. by 40 ft., may well belong to the period in which the yet vaster hall of William Rufus was rising close by.

[1] Customary, p. 196. The second part of this prohibition takes us back to the earlier chapter-house which was not so remote as the present one from the cloister; and it implies that the monks sat with open door so that they could see and be seen from the opposite side of the cloister. In the Customary of St Augustine's, Canterbury, which reproduces Abbot Richard de Ware's with certain necessary modifications, we find *juxta cameram abbatis* instead of *juxta celarium*: so that there the Abbot's Lodgings were at that time on the west side of the cloister, and the cellarer (as at Westminster later) was provided for elsewhere.

[2] Three sides of it are figured twice over, on pp. 416, 445, 446, and on plate xxxv at the end of the book. It was sold by Mr Capon, an antiquary, to Sir Gregory Page Turner, Bart., for one hundred guineas (*ibid.* p. 446). See further *Gilbert Crispin*, in this series, p. 35.

Though this capital is perhaps irrevocably lost, other capitals with somewhat similar sculptures happily remain, together with pillars and bases and the fragments of arches, discovered at various times and now brought together in the undercroft beneath the dormitory. When the ground of the cloister garth was lowered three feet and a half by Sir Gilbert Scott in 1869, a portion of the old cloister wall was revealed on the west side of the garth, and it can still be seen on the removal of a large stone cover which protects the walled trench which has been made to enclose it. It was noticed at the time that the upper stones bore marks which indicated the structures which rested upon them, but their interpretation was not properly made out. The reconstruction of the existing fragments in the undercroft suggests that the bases of the pillars are indicated by these marks, and so the exact distance between the pillars is ascertained. In April 1909 careful search was made for the foundations of this wall, and its line is now shewn by stones embedded in the grass[1].

Having thus dated the Norman cloister and noted its surrounding buildings, we are in a position to ask, Where was the abbot's *camera*? There is fortunately no doubt as to the answer. In the south-west angle of the cloister is an entrance chamber in line with the south walk. This served as the outer parlour (*locutorium extrinsecus*), where the monks spoke with their visitors. The chamber over it, which must have been reached by a newel stair, was the *camera* of the abbot. Although the parlour below was altered and modernised by Abbot Litlyngton in the fourteenth century, when the new cloister was being completed, the *camera* above shews sufficient indication of having existed in the earlier period: for its eastern wall partly overhangs the wall of the later cloister, and does not lie straight upon it, but is parallel with the old Norman wall in the cloister garth to which we have referred above.

The position thus assigned to the abbot's *camera* over the *locutorium* is borne out by the similar arrangement in the monastery of Gloucester; though, as the cloister there lies north of the church, these chambers are bounded on the south not by the refectory wall, but by the wall of the church itself. In later times this upper chamber was the prior's chapel, but originally it belonged to the abbot[2].

[1] See 'The Church of Edward the Confessor,' *Archaeologia*, vol. LXII, p. 94. The plan of the Abbey which I have there given will be found useful for the understanding of the present work.

[2] See Mr St John Hope's 'Notes on the Abbey of Gloucester,' *Archaeological Journal*, March, 1907.

It is possible that at the end of the eleventh century no further provision was made for the separate accommodation of the abbot. The Customary informs us that in ancient times (*antiquitus*) the abbot slept in the dormitory and dined in the refectory with his monks. But in the twelfth century the requirements of the abbot in the greater monasteries increased: his share of the monastic property was separated from that of the convent, and large duties of hospitality had to be discharged by him. Consequently he needed a hall and kitchen of his own.

Now an ancient wall on the south side of what afterwards came to be the abbot's courtyard has several small blocked windows high up, as well as traces of the relieving arches of larger openings on the ground floor. It is conceivable that this formed part of the north wall of the abbot's hall. The kitchen lies immediately to the west; so that, if this be its original position, we get the usual arrangement of the hall in the centre, the kitchen at one end, and the lord's *camera* at the other, reached by a door behind the dais or high table. If this supposition be correct, practically the whole of the twelfth-century house of the abbot still exists, though somewhat obscured by later modifications and additions.

Some confirmation of this view comes from the further consideration of a point which has been briefly alluded to already, and must now be examined more fully. The rebuilding of St Edward's church by King Henry III had included the choir and transepts, but had stopped short in the fourth bay west of the crossing. For the rest, the old Norman nave was linked on and left to do service for another hundred years. As for the cloister, the portions contiguous to the new church had been constructed in the new style; and in the course of the fourteenth century the remainder was by slow degrees rebuilt, until at last the cloister was finished in June 1365. The extension of the nave was of course in contemplation, though the old nave was not taken down until ten years after this date. But, when the measurements for its extension were calculated, it was plain that one of the buttresses supporting the fliers would stand out in the middle of the then existing west walk of the cloister. It was therefore necessary that this walk should be moved westward some five feet at its northern end, and that the whole range of the cellarer's buildings which bounded it should be demolished. A new west walk had to be constructed between two of the nave buttresses—sixteen feet and a half in width[1].

[1] For this and for what follows reference should be made to Plan, in cover.

At the southern end two points had to be taken into consideration in drawing the line of this new walk. First, the door of the refectory, which probably could not be shifted much to the west without great inconvenience; and, secondly, the abbot's *camera* over the outer parlour. Accordingly the line of the west wall was drawn from the buttress at the northern end to the eastern wall of the abbot's *camera*. This latter wall actually overhangs the new cloister wall a little, especially where they first meet: for it makes a right angle with the refectory wall, as did the old cloister wall, whereas the new wall makes an angle slightly obtuse (see Plan between pp. 6 and 7).

Now a careful measurement of the existing buildings of the abbot's house shews that a certain portion of them can be marked off from the rest by the fact that their lines run parallel or at right angles to the old west wall of the cloister: whereas all the buildings that are certainly new work of Litlyngton have a slightly different direction. The difference is indeed very small, and only reveals itself on a minute investigation. But it exists, and its existence confirms the belief that we are here dealing with work of an earlier period, and that this portion of the buildings formed the abbot's house of the Norman time.

The Turret Staircase.

If we go out on the leads over the room formerly called the High Dining-Room, but recently the Ante-Room, we may observe a slight irregularity in the parapet, nine feet from the tiled wall. Looking over, we see that the wall is set back here about three inches. We are in fact at the junction of the building which forms the south side of the courtyard and a small turret, nine feet square, which once contained a circular staircase.

The structure of this turret, of which almost every trace has now disappeared, is discoverable from the plans made for Dean Atterbury's alterations in 1715. It is there shewn as somewhat oddly cut away inside in order to make room for the ordinary wooden stairs. On the ground floor its eastern wall remains, and forms part of the west wall of the kitchen. An elevation of 1718 shews that it rose four feet above its present level and had a parapet on the top.

It must at one time have had a door leading by a landing to the west room over the entrance to the cloister and another lower down giving access to the Ante-Room, the floor of which is seven feet lower than that of the room just mentioned. It is possible that this turret-stair goes back to early Norman times, and was built to give access to the abbot's *camera*[1].

In the portion of the plan which is here reproduced the two rooms on the south, called 'Abbots Roome' and 'Landry,' are the rooms over the entrance to the cloister. The 'Abbots Roome' is certainly the most ancient part of the house; and it is interesting to find the tradition that this was the original *camera* of the abbot lingering on into the eighteenth century. 'My L^ds^ Bedchamber' is the room over the present dining-room. The staircase was more or less straightened (see Plan of First Floor), probably as the result of the changes which this plan was drawn to prepare for: so that the circle of the *vise* can no longer be traced.

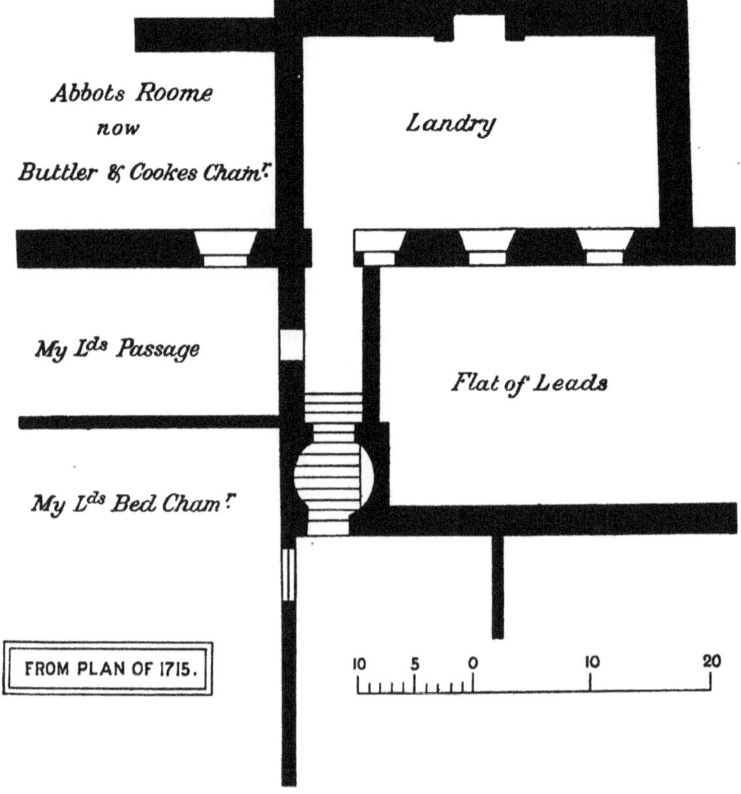

[1] There is a deeply recessed wall to the south of this turret, forming part of the east wall of the coal-cellar. A good deal of alteration has taken place at this point, and I am not able satisfactorily to account for it.

The Deanery Westminster.

Plan of part of 1st Floor shewing the Angle of Norman building as compared with the later work.

Scale 1/8" inch = 1 foot.

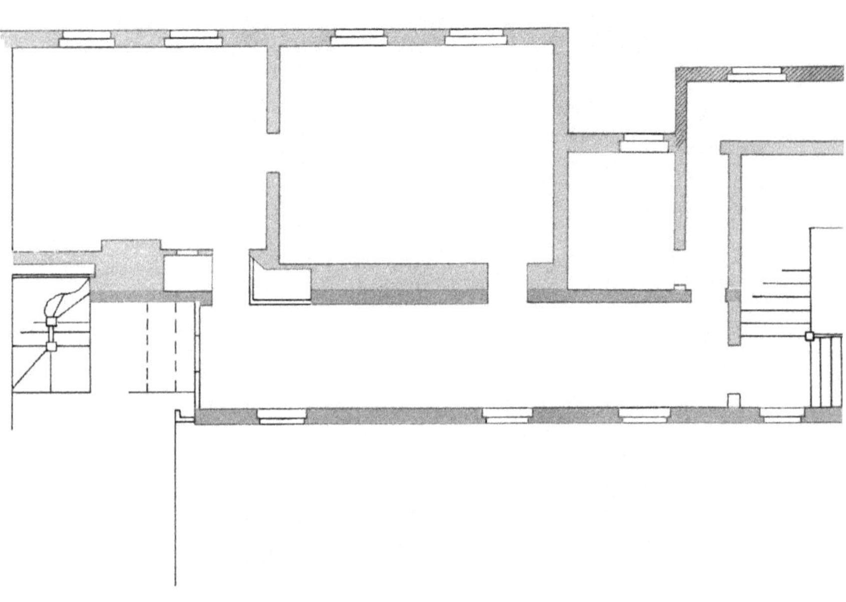

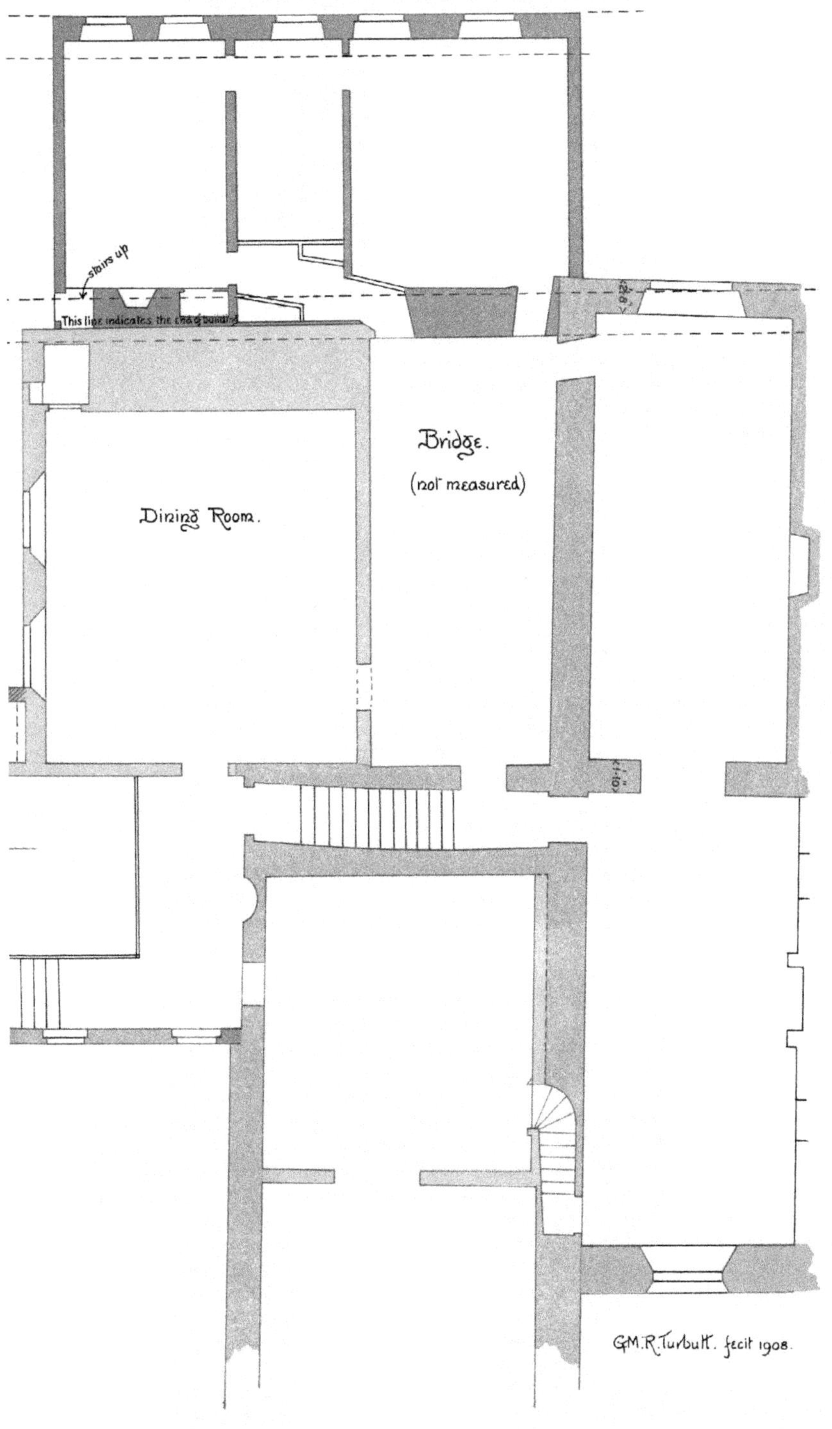
stairs up
This line indicates the end of building
2'8"
Bridge.
(not measured)
Dining Room.
1'10"
G.M.R. Turbutt. fecit 1908.

An earlier building on the site of Jerusalem Chamber.

The eastern wall of Jerusalem Chamber is nearly, but not quite, contiguous with the western face of the south-west tower, and where the recess of the tower comes a deep pit is formed between the two buildings, which is a favourite nesting-place of the abbey pigeons. If we look down into this pit, we may see two sets of corbels on the wall of Jerusalem, which now serve no purpose at all. It seems impossible to interpret them otherwise than by the supposition that they belonged to a chamber east of Jerusalem, which had to be pulled down to make room for the new towers of the extended nave.

In the passage which leads from the present servants' hall to the cellars under Jerusalem we find in the southern wall similar corbels a little below the level of the lower of the two sets above mentioned. These also are at present without employment; but at some period subsequent to the building of the tower they seem to have been used to carry the joists of an upper passage.

When we look at a plan which shews Jerusalem Chamber and the abbot's hall, we see that the walls of the former are considerably thicker, with the exception of the east wall, which on our supposition was not originally intended for an external wall. The wall in the passage which contains the corbels is three feet thick; and it contains a window of quite a different type from the windows in the long passage under the gallery.

We conclude therefore that before Litlyngton began his work of reconstruction there existed a building on this site, which was about twice the size of the present building, though probably its upper chambers were not so lofty as Jerusalem now is. The eastern half of this, except its southern wall, had to be pulled down in order to make room for the south-west tower. But the western half was saved, and its upper portion was renewed and beautified as the *nova camera* of the abbot, intended to form the solar at the back of the dais of his new hall. This work of reconstruction was completed, as we shall presently see, some three years before the old nave was pulled down; and we may perhaps assume that the extent of the new nave and its western towers had already been carefully calculated[1].

[1] A careful examination of the walls of Jerusalem Chamber and the hall bears out the general conclusions drawn above. The west wall of Jerusalem is 4′ 6″ in thickness, the south wall 4′ 7″ (the present difference being doubtless due to the protected position of the latter, which has saved it from decay); the walls of Litlyngton's hall are 3′ 1″ or 3′ 2″.

It is very probable that the building which was thus partially demolished ran right up to the Norman south-west tower. I am now inclined to extend the Norman nave two bays further to the west than in the conjectural plan which I appended to my study of the Church of Edward the Confessor[1]; for this makes it easier to understand the letter in which Litlyngton informed Simon Langham that he had everything in readiness 'for the length of three pillars' early in 1376; and it also provides a more reasonable size for the old nave which had been left and joined on to Henry III's new work a hundred years before.

An outside view of the west walls of Jerusalem and the hall seems at first sight to suggest that all was built at one time: the lower part not only shews no break at all where the buildings join, but also is ornamented by a continuous band of bricks and flints. But higher up above the windows (which have been restored) it is plain that the present face of the wall of the hall shews the ancient stones, now much decayed; whereas its lower part and also the wall of Jerusalem have been refaced in modern times. It is reasonable to suppose that the wall which still shews the old work is of a *later* date than the wall which forty years ago needed to be entirely refaced.

The south wall of Jerusalem has been protected on its south face by the Chapter wine-cellar, and its appearance is instructive. It is easy to observe the difference in construction between it and the walls of Litlyngton's hall, east and west. It shews a considerable number of evenly laid small square blocks, suggesting that it was once an external wall carefully built though afterwards a good deal patched: and it also has a good deal of chalk in it.

The 3-ft. wall which continues this south wall towards the east is not quite parallel with the base of the tower, being nearer to it by a foot at its eastern end. It is the wall referred to above as containing some of the corbels. I think there can be no doubt that it is earlier than the tower base, though it may not be so early as the thick walls of Jerusalem, unless indeed it was not originally built as an external wall. When Islip erected his new building he built parallel or at right angles to this wall, not to the tower base.

[1] *Archaeologia*, LXII, 81—100 (1910).

II. THE WORK OF ABBOT LITLYNGTON.

John Flete, who was prior from 1448—65, wrote a history of the Abbey which ends with the year of Abbot Litlyngton's death, namely 1386. He informs us that 'in this abbot's time and by his industrious activity there were built anew from the foundations the whole of the abbot's place next the church, half the cloister (namely its western and southern sides), the offices of some of the obedientiaries (as the bailiff's, the infirmarer's, the sacrist's and the cellarer's), the great malthouse with the tower there, the water-mill and the dam with walls of stone, as well as the stone enclosure of the infirmary garden: all of which were built out of the property of the church, and specially out of the property of Simon de Langham his predecessor, to the great honour of the monastery aforesaid[1].'

Various account-rolls are preserved which bear out this statement in general; but we shall find that the latter portion of it is not applicable to the rebuilding of the abbot's house, the payments for which came out of Litlyngton's own purse[2]. The rebuilding of the cellarer's department was, as we have already seen, necessitated by the alteration of the line of the west cloister walk. The cellarer was housed in convenient buildings close to the convent kitchen: they still remain, and are occupied as dwelling-houses, on the east side of what is now Dean's Yard.

The site at Litlyngton's disposal for the abbot's place, after the removal of the cellarer's buildings, may be roughly described as an oblong of about 130 by 260 feet. It was bounded on the east by the cloister, and on the north by a line drawn from the cloister wall past the south-west tower as far as the great gatehouse, which stood until 1777 nearly where the Crimean Memorial now stands in the Great Sanctuary. This oblong was divided by Litlyngton's new hall into two squares, the western of which was left free for a garden. The square between the hall and the cloister was itself divided by a gallery which

[1] Flete's *History of Westminster Abbey*, p. 135: see below, *Illustrative Documents*, A.

[2] See below, *Illustr. Doc.* B.

ran across to the south-east corner of the tower: the two sub-divisions thus formed were the abbot's courtyard and the little garden under the cloister wall[1].

We are fortunate in possessing a series of Abbot Litlyngton's account-rolls, which enable us to trace with some exactness the progress of his building operations. When Litlyngton became abbot in April 1362, he made John Lakyngheth, an able young monk, warden of his household (*custos hospicii*) and abbot's treasurer—for he bears both titles[2]. But in 1371 Lakyngheth became treasurer to the convent, and after that the abbot was less fortunate in his managers. A clerk of the kitchen, one Richard Fortheye, now presents the accounts; but the abbot gets into debt. Presently William Colchester, who succeeded Litlyngton as abbot, appears as treasurer and warden of the household. From 1374 Fortheye presents a portion of the accounts as clerk of the kitchen, and the treasurer presents a separate roll: but in March 1379, Fortheye hands over his task to William de Greseleye, who is styled seneschal of the household; and shortly afterwards other arrangements are made.

These rolls, besides being important for the study of the domestic economy of the latter part of the fourteenth century, contain here and there points of extraordinary interest. Gardeners will be pleased to find a payment made at the abbot's manor of Denham to a boy who brought 'plants of Wardon pears' from Hendon in 1368. The abbot was engaged on great building operations at Denham at that time. But we see him not only as a builder, but also as a lover of the chase. In 1369 a collar is bought for a harrier named Sturdy; and there are many references to his dogs and horses. But the most remarkable entry is that which in 1368 immediately follows certain payments for his chapel: the sum of sixpence is paid 'for one falcon of wax to be offered for a sick falcon.' Whether the abbot approved of such methods of healing or not, the entry remains unchallenged by his auditor[3].

From these accounts we are able to trace the general course of operations. From 1362 to 1365 work is going on above the entrance to the cloister, and payments are made to John Mordon, who was *custos*

[1] See Plan in cover.

[2] See below, *Illustr. Doc.* B. For an account of John Lakyngheth see 'An Unrecognised Westminster Chronicler,' *Proceedings of British Academy*, 1907, vol. III, pp. 15—17.

[3] 1367—8 (*Munim.* 24,512): 'Et in j falcon' de cer' emp' pro j falcon' infirm' offerend'. vj d....et cuidam garcioni venient' de Hendon cum plantis pirarum Wardonum apud Denham precepto domini. vj d.'

1368—9 (*Munim.* 24,513): 'In j colar' emp' pro Sturdy leporar' precepto domini. iij d.

novi operis and was then engaged upon the cloister which was finished in 1365.

Two rolls are missing, but in 1367—8 the abbot pays to Walter Warfeld the cellarer £20 towards the new gate of the abbey at the western end of his site.

The roll for 1369—70 is missing, but for nine years after that payments are made to Walter Warfeld for what is called *novum edificium*. In 1371—2 canvas is bought for the windows of 'my lord's new *camera*': and, as we have elsewhere a mention of the wall from the gate of the abbey to the abbot's *camera*, there is no doubt that Jerusalem Chamber is here referred to. After this the abbot's hall was built, and an account-roll of Walter Warfeld shews us that in 1375—6 it was so far finished that John Payable was putting in the glass—of which a fragment bearing the initials N.L. still remains in its place. After 1379 the payments for *novum edificium* cease.

In 1380—1 a small payment is made to William Mordon 'in aid of the wall next the gate.' We shall see presently that this wall had been built at the abbot's cost, and that William Mordon was now putting on the battlements.

One thing remained to be done, but it was not undertaken at once. This was to provide a covered way by which the abbot could reach Jerusalem Chamber without having to go through the hall. In 1383—4 foundations were being laid in the garden, and the next year a gallery was made across from the southern side of the court to the east end of the base of the new tower, and thence along its south face to Jerusalem Chamber. This is called 'the little cloister within the abbot's mansion,' and also 'the Aley.' The lower passage was built of stone and remains almost intact: the upper passage was, as now, of lath and plaster, but parts of it have been swallowed up in subsequent enlargements of the house.

Two incidental references to Litlyngton's new buildings may be noted here. They are both found in the *Liber Niger Quaternus*, a fifteenth century chartulary compiled from earlier books and containing a series of notes written at the end of the fourteenth century by a monk who was contemporary with Abbot Litlyngton.

Here we are told that 'Walter Warfelde the cellarer caused both the gates of Tothull to be made at his own costs and charges; but Nicholas Litlyngton the abbot made for twenty pounds the wall between the abbot's *camera* and the prison; and William Mordon, the warden of the works, afterwards furnished the said wall with battlements.' The author of this paragraph could not fill in the exact year of King Edward III's reign: but by comparing the abbot's and cellarer's accounts we can gather that this wall was built in 1367—8, that is to say, four years before the abbot's new *camera* was completed. The date offers no difficulty now that we know that the new *camera* was only a reconstruction and not an entirely fresh piece of building[1].

The other reference is a gossiping story of the cloister, which we must hope is pátient of a less sinister interpretation than our author puts upon it. When his house was built, the abbot asked the prior and convent to let him have some of the lead which had come off the old part of the church to roof in his new buildings, and he promised not to forget the favour when occasion should arise. Now it happened that monies came from abroad as part of Simon Langham's legacy, and were deposited in the vestry under two keys, one of which was held by the abbot, and the other by some person unnamed—presumably another executor. This treasure was needed and used; but the convent were not aware of it, and accordingly having need of money they proposed to the abbot that they should be allowed to have some of this in return for their lead. The abbot cheerfully acquiesced; but, when Richard Merston the prior came with the brethren to get it, they found no more than a hundred shillings. So were they frustrated and deceived, and got nothing for their lead unto this day[2].

[1] *Lib. Nig.* f. 79 *b*: '*De Porta Abbathie versus Tothull, etc.* Anno regni regis Edwardi tertii...usque...Frater Walterus Warfelde Celararius fieri fecit utramque portam de Tothull cum pertinentibus sumptibus suis et expensis: sed dn̄s Nicholaus Litlyngton Abbas de xxli. fecit murum inter Cameram Abbatis et prisonam: Willelmus Mordon custos operis postea dictum murum embatilavit.'

Comp. Walcott, *Memorials of Westminster*, p. 273: 'The Gatehouse, once the principal approach to the monastery, stood at the western entrance of Tothill-street, and consisted of two gates,—the southern leading out of Great Dean's Yard, a receptacle for felons. On the east side was the Bishop of London's prison for Clerks-convict; and the rooms over the other gate adjoining, but towards the west, were for offenders committed from the Liberties or City of Westminster.' This Gatehouse was pulled down in 1777.

The next entry in the *Liber Niger* shews that Abbot Litlyngton was only rebuilding a former Gatehouse, which had also served as a prison. It is a summary of a grant by Simon Langham confirming to Agnes Crips a grant, formerly made without the abbot's knowledge or consent, of a piece of land next the gaol, reserving eight feet square for a *via de gradibus ibidem ponendis* for bringing in and out felons: dated 5 Mar. 24 Edw. III.

[2] *Lib. Nig.* f. 80 *b*. See below, *Illustr. Doc.* D.

III. SUBSEQUENT DEVELOPMENTS.

The stately mansion thus completed by Abbot Litlyngton remained unaltered, so far as we can tell, for the next hundred years. An interesting reference to it occurs in Abbot Esteney's time (1474—98). Elizabeth Wydville, the queen of Edward IV, had taken sanctuary here on two occasions. And on the accession of Henry VII the widowed queen obtained a lease of the house from the abbot; but whether she entered into possession may be questioned, as she was soon afterwards sent to the abbey of Bermondsey, where she died in 1492. The house is described in the lease as the mansion of Cheynegates[1].

From 1500 to 1532 John Islip was abbot, and by him, if tradition be true, the first important addition was made. He constructed a set of chambers, two storeys high, on the north side of the courtyard, swallowing up a portion of Litlyngton's gallery, but not removing its substructures. This new building, which includes Jericho Parlour and the rooms above and below, he carried round the east side of the tower, making chambers between it and the first buttress of the nave, and opening an oriel window into the church itself. To Islip also we must attribute a modification of the entrance archway leading into the courtyard; for its somewhat peculiar vaulting, with plain round bosses, closely corresponds to that of the gateway of the Bloody Tower in the Tower of London, which belongs to the early part of the sixteenth century.

At the Dissolution the abbot's house was granted to the newly constituted bishop of Westminster. His grant, which is dated 20 Jan. 1541, contains an interesting description of the house with various measurements of its extent[2]. The former abbot, William Boston, who now, as William Benson, became the first dean, found a residence in what had been, as we shall see, the prior's house, south of the refectory, on the site where Ashburnham House now stands[3].

The bishopric of Westminster lasted no more than ten years, and when Bishop Thirlby removed to Norwich the abbot's place passed into lay hands. It was granted on 30 May 1550, to Lord Wentworth, a first cousin of the Protector Somerset. Lord Wentworth died in March 1551,

[1] See below, *Illustr. Doc.* E. [2] *Ibid.* F.

[3] The site of the prior's house is discussed below, *ibid.* H.

and the house came to his son, the second Lord Wentworth, soon to become notorious for the surrender of Calais.

The return of the monks under Abbot Feckenham at the end of 1556 involved the ejection of the lay proprietor, who was compensated with the manor of Canonbury: his surrender is dated 31 May 1557. But for this short-lived restoration of the abbot it is possible that the house would still be occupied to-day by some noble or wealthy intruder.

Queen Elizabeth gave back the entire site of the abbey to the dean and chapter by a charter dated 21 May 1560, and thereupon the abbot's house became the deanery. The earlier deans—Bill, Goodman and Andrews—appear to have made no structural changes; but in 1606 Dean Neile built 'for the bettering of the Deane's lodginge' a small building next to Islip's over the north end of the gallery. It contained two chambers made of lath and plaster like the gallery itself. The portion of it which was directly above the gallery still remains as a diminutive bedroom: the rest was lost in a further reconstruction more than a century later[1].

The year 1550 had seen the bishop disappear and the house pass to Lord Wentworth: in 1650 the dean had disappeared and the house had passed to 'Lord Bradshawe.' In a paper bearing his signature and dated '22° 10bre 1652' he says: 'I was settled there by the Parliament at the tryall of the King and Lords, and was tenant in possession when the Governors were appointed.' Nevertheless he had to come to terms with 'the Governors of the School and Almshouses of the late Colledge of Westminster,' who had succeeded to the dean and prebendaries, and who were determined to get a fair rent for what is described in his lease as 'the Colledge, or the late Deane's house[2].'

Although little of his work remains quite as he left it, Bradshaw made considerable alterations and additions, expending the large sum of £760. From his lease we learn that he not only occupied the 'Tower Chamber,' which still bears his name, at the end of the south triforium of the church, but also built rooms 'upon the Two Towers adjoining to the said Church.' This puzzling statement is at once explained when we look at a drawing by King in the first edition of Dugdale's *Monasticon*, where we see what appear to be two wooden boxes with a bridge between them on the south-east and south-west turrets of the unfinished south-west tower. We further gather from the lease that he occupied the lodgings over the south-west corner of the cloister, formerly in the tenure of the late Mr Pay the auditor; and the house opposite, over

[1] See below, *Illustr. Doc.* J. nos. 1—8, 23, 24.

[2] *Ibid.* J. nos. 18—20.

the east cloister walk, part of which came down within the cloister garth. The former of these, which is mentioned in the grant to Bishop Thirlby and was reconstructed by Dean Williams, has since remained incorporated in the deanery[1]; the latter was pulled down in the eighteenth century.

The bills of the workmen shew us that Bradshaw built a new kitchen, turning the old one into a servants' dining-room; and that he constructed a new dining-room and a great staircase. Subsequent changes have made it difficult to identify the whole of his work with exactness, but it is plain that he must have vastly increased the comfort of the house. His wife died in it about the end of 1655, and he followed her on 22 Nov. 1659, six months before the king's return.

Dean Sprat in 1683 built a new room off the gallery, and Atterbury, his successor (1713—23), added a similar room to the north of it, destroying in the process a portion of the chambers built a century before by Dean Neile. These two rooms, which have for long been known as the Red Rooms, are the last addition made to the house. Atterbury did further service in rescuing from an almost ruinous state the two rooms over the entrance to the cloister, one of which then bore the name of the 'Abbots Roome now Butler and Cookes Chamber,' while the other, west of it, was called the 'Landry[2].' Some fine decorative work belongs to the period of Dean Wilcocks (1731—1756), and some modern conveniences were added by Dean Bradley (1881—1902).

A gallery with chambers connected with it, running west from Jerusalem Chamber towards the Gatehouse, has wholly disappeared. It existed before the Dissolution and apparently until the latter part of the eighteenth century[3]. With this exception the old house of the abbots, as Litlyngton rebuilt it and Islip enlarged it, remains in its completeness to-day, although portions of it are obscured by the later structures which have grown up about it in the following centuries.

[1] These rooms are traditionally called the Tudor Rooms: that they are of yet earlier date is shewn by a reference to their repairs in 1482—3 (*in repar' unius domus ex parte occidentali dicti claustri et factur' unius novi guttur' ibidem*). See Mr Rackham's 'Nave of Westminster,' *Proc. of Brit. Acad.* vol. IV, p. 39: and note also a reference to Cheynygates, *ibid.* p. 45 *n.*

[2] Plan of 1715: but in the plan of 1718 they are called respectively 'Library' and 'Anty Chamber.'

[3] Reference to this gallery is made below, *Illustr. Doc.* J. no. 25. This is probably the gallery in which Lord Keeper Williams had an interview with the Spanish ambassador's secretary, as described by Bishop Hacket in his *Life of Williams*, I. 198: 'with a seeming unwillingness it was allowed him, keeping a cautious limit, not to make his Visit till Eleven of the Clock that Night, and by the back door of the Garden, where a Servant should receive him. He came at his hour, and being brought into a Gallery,' &c.

IV. ILLUSTRATIVE DOCUMENTS AND NOTES.

A.

Flete's Description of Litlyngton's Building Operations.

Hujus abbatis tempore et industria aedificata sunt a fundamentis de novo tota placea abbatis juxta ecclesiam; dimidium autem claustri ex partibus occidente et australi; domus quorumdam officiariorum, ut puta ballivi, infirmarii, sacristae et celerarii; magnum malthous cum turri ibidem; molendinum aquaticum et le dam cum muris lapideis, cum clausura lapidea gardini infirmariae (*Hist. of Westm.* p. 135).

B.

Summaries and Specimens from Litlyngton's Accounts.

1. *Summary of payments for the Abbot's House.*

Year	Work	Payment	Total
1362—3		*	
1363—4	Work above cloister	15 · 0 · 0	29 · 8 · 7
1364—5	(paid to John Mordon)	14 · 8 · 7	
—		. . .	
—		. . .	
1367—8	Work about great gate	20 · 0 · 0	20 · 0 · 0
1368—9	(paid to Walter Warfeld)	*	
—		. . .	
1370—1		42 · 0 · 8	
1371—2		118 · 0 · 0	
1372—3		80 · 6 · 3	
1373—4		41 · 12 · 4	
1374—5	*Novum edificium* (paid to Walter Warfeld)	2 · 1 · 10	
—		. . .	
—		. . .	
1377—8		31 · 10 · 0	
1378—9		19 · 9 · 7	335 · 8 · 0
1379—80	(*nil*)	. . .	
1380—1	Towards wall next great gate (paid to William Mordon)	3 · 6 · 8	3 · 6 · 8
—		. . .	
1382—3	(*nil*)	. . .	
1383—4	Little cloister, or Aley	5 · 11	
1384—5	(paid to William Mordon and Richard Tournor)	66 · 6 · 11½	66 · 13 · 10½

The years run from Michaelmas to Michaelmas. The asterisks indicate years in which mention is made only of gratuities to workmen engaged on the work in question. In the rolls preserved for 1379—80 and 1382—3 no payments are made for the work. For six years out of the twenty-three the rolls are missing.

In 1375—6 (*Munim.* 18,858) Walter Warfeld the cellarer renders account shewing that out of £145. 16*s.* received by him he has spent £101. 8*s.* 5*d.* (see below, p. 19).

2. *Extracts relating to Litlyngton's building operations.*

1362—3. John Lakyngheth, *Custos hospicii* (*Munim.* 24,510).

Item dat' operantibus in camera super claustrum apud Westm' precepto domini. vjd.

1363—4. J. L., *Thesaurarius abbatis* (24,261).

Et fratri J. Murdon pro factura novi edificii juxta claustrum. xvli. per tall'.

Et servienti de Denham pro factura novi edificii ibidem. xxxli. vs. vjd.

Et preposito de Periford pro emendacione aule et camerarum ibidem. xli. xiijs. viijd.

1364—5. J. L., *Custos hospicii* (24,511).

Et J. Mordon pro factura operis in introitu claustri. cs.

Et eidem pro factura dicti operis per manus domini. ixli. viijs. vijd.

Et Roberto Broun servienti de Denham per tall' pro factura novi edificii. xxjli. iijs. ijd.

1367—8. J. L., *Custos hospicii* (24,512).

Et comp' se liberasse Roberto Broun servienti de Denham, ut in diversis custibus factis circa novam edificacionem ibidem, et circa clausuram parci, et in denariis, ut patet per parcell'. lvjli. xijs. vijd. ob. per tall'.

Et supradicto fratri Waltero Warfeld pro opere nove porte Abathie. xxli.

1368—9. J. L., *Custos hospicii* (24,513).

Et dat' fabro apud portam abbathie Westm' precepto domini. iiijd.

(Spent on Denham—domus, pons, fossa—£92.)

1370—1. J. L., *Custos hospicii* (24,514).

Et comp' se liberasse fratri Waltero de Warefeld precepto domini pro opere novi edificii apud Westm'. xlijli. viijd.

1371 (vigil of Mich. to 26 Oct.). J. L., *Thesaurarius abbatis* (24,514 B).

Et Waltero Warefeld pro opere novi edificii apud Westm'. xviijli.

1371—2. Richard Fortheye, *Clericus coquinae* (24,515).

Et in v ulnis de canafas emp' pro fenestr' nove camere domini apud Westm', precio ulne. vd. ob., ijs. iijd. ob.

Et dat' cementario apud Westm' precepto domini. iijs. iiijd.

Et lib' fratri Waltero de Warefeld pro novo edificio apud Westm'. cli. per tall'.

1372—3. Richard Fortheye, *Clericus coquinae* (24,516).

Et lib' fratri Waltero Warefeld pro edificacione apud Westm' per ij tall'. iiij^xx^ti. vjs. iijd.

1373—4. William Colchester, *Custos hospicii* (24,517).

Et ortolano Westm' causa laboris sui in novo edificio domini ibidem. iijs. iiijd.

Et lib' fratri Waltero Warfeld pro nova edificacione apud Westm', ut patet per parcellas. xjti. xijs. iiijd.

Et lib' Waltero Warfeld pro dicto novo edificio per manus domini. xxti.

Et lib' eidem Waltero Warfeld. xti.

1374—5. Richard Fortheye, *Clericus coquinae* (24,518).

Item lib' fratri Waltero Warfeld in cariac° meremii usque Westm'. xljs. xd.

1377—8. *Thesaurarius abbatis* (24,520).

Et fratri Waltero Warfeld pro novo edificio apud Westm'. xxxjti. xs.

1378—9. *Thesaurarius abbatis* (24,521).

Et fratri Waltero Warfeld pro novo edificio apud Westm'. xixti. ixs. vijd.

1380—1. *Thesaurarius abbatis* (24,528).

Et fratri Willelmo Mordon in auxilio muri juxta portam Westm'. lxvjs. viijd.

1383—4. *Thesaurarius abbatis* (24,532).

Et eidem [sc. Willelmo Mordon] pro uno novo fundamento in gard' Westm'. vs. xjd.

1384—5. *Thesaurarius abbatis* (24,532* D).

Et solut' R. Tournor tam pro factura parvi claustri infra mansionem abbatis quam pro meremio ad idem. xxvti. preter robam suam precio xjs. vijd. ex convencione. et solut' ij hominibus latthantibus dictum claustrum. ixs. ijd. in dorenayl', wyndownayl', lathenall' empt' ad idem. xxviijs. xid. ob. et solut' dalbator' pro dalbac' et pargettac' murorum et aree dicti claustri in grosso, una cum potac' post prandium. ljs. et solut' pro xxvj carect' argill' cum cariag' ejusdem. vjs. vjd. in di^c^[1] calc' adust' empt' pro opere predicto. iijs. et solut' fratri Willelmo Mordon pro petris et factura duorum hostiorum ad utrumque finem dict' Aley, in iij paribus vertynell' cum iij serruris et clavibus, latthes et aliis appendiciis empt' ad idem. xxs. in m^l^ hertlatthes empt' preter illa que Ric. Tournour invenit. vjs. viijd. et solut' pro vj waiis plumbi j quartron. xxxiijti. vjs. viijd. et solut' pro lti. soudur'. xxvs.

Summa...........lxvjti. vjs. xjd. ob.

These extracts shew us that in 1364 the abbot was engaged in building another house at Denham. The work went on till 1369 and cost him £150 in the years for which accounts are preserved. We find

[1] I.e. half a hundred.

him residing there in 1375—6, at the time of his correspondence with Simon Langham at Avignon regarding the rebuilding of the nave of the church.

It appears then that, having set in order the abbot's *camera* over the new entrance to the cloister, he proceeded to build his great manor-house at Denham, and then in 1370 began his *novum edificium* at Westminster which took nine years to build, and which cost him, if we make allowance for several missing rolls, about £450.

The following is the account of Walter Warfeld to which reference has already been made.

Munim. 18,859 (1375—6).

Compotus fratris Walteri de Warfeld celerarii Westm' de omnibus receptis et expensis operis domini abbatis Westm' a festo sancti Michaelis anno xlix° usque idem festum anno quinquagesimo.

Rec' den'. In primis r' de iiij^{xx}li. rec' de abbate per unam talliam. Et de xls. rec' de domino Johanne de Blockele sine tallia. Et de xixli. xixs. iiijd. rec' de fratre Johanne Lakynghyt ballivo pro lan' domini sine tallia. Et de xxvjs. viijd. rec' pro lan'[1] angn'[2]. Et de xxli. rec' de domino priore sine tallia. Et de vjli. rec' de Waltero Page de arr' suo per[3] talliam. Et de vijli. rec' de Willelmo Carter nuper ballivo de la Hyde per[3] talliam. Et de xs. rec' de pomis de la curtyl hoc anno venditis. Et ixli. rec' de Willelmo Carter nuper ballivo de la Hyde de arr' suo sine tallia.

Summa recepte cxlvli. xvjs.

Expens'.

Empcio lapidum. In primis solut' pro iiij^{or} batell' de Ragg' emp' cvjs. viijd. prec' batell' xxvjs. viijd. Et in ij batell' lapid' de Reygate emp' iiijli. Et in car' per aquam iiijs. Et in una batell' de calc' emp' xiijs. iiijd. Et[4] de iij batell' lapid' de Reygate rec' de Willelmo Mordon nil quia in comp' ejusdem Willelmi[5]. Et solut' pro car' vjs.

Summa xli. xs.

Cementar'. Et solut' Johanni Mason per x septimanas xxxvjs. viijd. cap' per septimanam iijs. viijd. Et solut' alio cementario conducto per xxj diem[6] pro cap' fact' in aula[7] xxjs. cap' per diem xijd. Et in emendacione instrumentorum cementar' et cubitor' per vices xxd.

Summa lixs. iiijd.

Cubitor'. Et solut' ij cubitor'[8] per xj septimanas operantibus super murum juxta gardinum et in aliis locis[9] lxxiijs. iiijd. cuilibet per septimanam iijs. iiijd.

A = *Mun.* 18,858, *the first draft of this account.*

1 lanis A. 2 angn = agninis (?). 3 per] + unam A. 4 Et *cancelled.*

5 nil—Willelmi] *inserted between the lines* : *om.* A. 6 diem] *so also* A.

7 aula] + domini A. 8 cubitor'] + conduct' *added between lines* A.

9 locis] + necessariis *added between lines* A.

Et in ij labor' conduct' per xj septimanas operantibus cum cubitoribus xxxvjs. viijd. cuilibet per septimanam xxd. Et in alio labor' conduct' per iij septimanas pro mundacione mur' aule vs. cap' per septimanam xxd. Et in dcccc et di' calc' adust' emp'[1] lxiijs. iiijd. prec' c vjs. viiijd.

Summa viijli. xviijs. iiijd.

Carpent'. Et solut' diversis carpent' conduct' pro factura aule xlixli. xs. ixd. Et in ccc de estrichebord' emp' lxxs. vjd. prec' c xxiijs. vjd. Et in cc de estrichebord' emp' xlviijs. viijd. prec' c xxiiijs. iiijd. Et in ij Rygoldbordys emp' xvjd. Et in mmmd clav'[2] emp' pro aula xxvjs. iijd. prec' c ixd. Et in c clav' emp' pro aliis necessariis factis vjd. Et in mmmm de parvis clav' emp' pro aula xiijs. iiijd. prec' c iiijd. Et in soundys emp' xiiijd. Et in[3] ij sarrator' conduct' per liij dies et di' lxjs. xjd. cap' per diem xiiijd. Et solut' pro mdccclxvj pedibus de bordys sarrand' per vices xxiiijs. viijd. cap'[4] pro c xvjd. Et solut' Willelmo Wyntryngham vijli. Et in xiiij paribus ceroticar' emp' pro carpent' ijs. iiijd. Et in carn' emp' pro dictis carpent' iijs. vjd. Et in carn' piss' emp' pro Willelmo Wyntryngham per vices iijs. iiijd.

Summa lxixli. viijs. iijd.

Custus dom'. In primis solut' Johanni Payable vitriator' pro fenestris vitriat' in aula viijli. Et solut' pro j pari hengys pro ostio juxta ostium coquine xijd. Et in ij hokys emp' pro dicto ostio iiijd. Et in ij hokys emp' pro ostio juxta ostium gardini iiijd. Et in iij barwys emp' iiijs. Et in ij tribul' emp' xviijd.

Summa viijli. vijs. ijd.[5]

Expens' forinsec'. Et solut'......[6] pro car' meremii a Pyreford usque Westm' xxd. Et solut' pro lavacione de ledhassyn xs. Et solut' pro car' unius hauke a sancta Katerina usque Westm' pro la vermin per aquam iiijd.

Summa xijs.

Pitanc'. Et solut' pro pitanc' sancti Nicholai xiijs. iiijd.

Summa xiijs. iiijd.

Summa totalis expens' cjli. viijs. vd. Et debet xliiijli. vijs. vijd.

C.

The Six Oaks requested for the Abbot by the King.

Cambridge University Library, MS Dd. 3. 53, p. 93.

¶ De donacione maeremii. Trescher en dieu. Autrefoiz pur la necessite quel nostre cher en dieu labbe de Westmonster qest en fesant vne Sale de nouel en labbacie de Westmonster ad de sys triefs appelles bemes pur la dite Sale et nad en nulle de ses boys ne ne poet

[1] emp']+pro cubitor' A. [2] mangn' clav' (=magnis clavis) A. [3] in] solut' A.
[4] *om.* cap' A. [5] *The rest of this roll is missing: what follows is from* A.
[6] *A proper name is here cancelled.*

trouer nulle part es parties enuiron sys tieles arbres cheisnes come busoignent pur les triefs auantditz sicome il nous ad certeinement dit vous priasmes que vous lui vorriez eider de sys tieles arbres en vn vostre boys expressez es ditz lettres. Et porce que nous nauons puis †ou (? ouir) si vous eiez parfaite nostre dite priere ou nemie, Vous de rechief especialment et de cuer que vous lui veullez eider de sys tieux triefs en vostre dit boys par la cause auantdite pur amour de nous et par consideracion de noz prieres. En quel chose fesant vous nous ferrez plein plesir, paront nous vous volons sauoir bone gree. Si vous veullez certifier par voz lettres par le portour de cestes de ce que vous eut veullez faire. don' etc.

This letter comes from a Formulary, or book of examples—a Complete Letter-writer—which contains many items which clearly belong to the time of King Richard II. The king requests an unnamed correspondent to give the abbot of Westminster six oaks from his wood, also unnamed, for the beams of his new hall. We can hardly doubt that the abbot is Nicholas Litlyngton.

The scribe has evidently not understood the meaning of what he wrote. For this transcript I am indebted to Mr Alfred Rogers of the University Library.

D.

THE STORY OF THE LEAD LENT TO THE ABBOT.

De plumbo prestito abbati N. L. per conventum et non restaurato. Item circa idem tempus dn̄s Nicholaus Litelton tunc abbas Westm', cum perfecisset structuram edificii sui novi in placea sua apud Westm', peciit a conventu habere partem plumbi veteris ecclesie ad operiendum edificium suum novum, promittens eis quod in aliis postmodum agendis proficere vellet conventui in valore talionis &c. erat enim idem dn̄s abbas unus de executoribus testamenti dn̄i Simonis dudum cardinalis: qui videlicet dn̄s cardinalis paulo ante obitum suum multa bona legavit conventui et ecclesie Westm': ac inter cetera quidam transmarinus et alii attulerant ad Westm' per vices in denariis thesaurum ad summam ducentarum librarum, que reposite fuerunt in vestibulo Westm' sub duobus clavibus, unde una fuit in custodia dicti Nicholai L. abbatis et alia in custodia dicti......cumque speraret conventus habere illam summam quia de motione et voluntate dicti N. L. abbatis concesserunt eidem plumbum ecclesie supradictum ad operimentum novi edificii sui. quod cum factum fuisset dicti executores prefati cardinalis statuto quodam die venerunt et acceperunt thesaurum predictum nesciente conventu. et cum quadam die prior et conventus Westm' pecierunt dn̄m̄ N. L. abbatem pro quibusdam negociis suis subsidium et relevamen habere de pecuniis in thesauro cardinalis—quod cum dictus abbas unus executor libenter eis annueret, venerunt prior Ricardus Merston <et conventus> sperantes ibidem pecunias habuisse; sed tamen omnino frustrati sunt et decepti. nam infra cistam thesauri predicti vix invenierunt C.s. et sic nil habuerunt pro toto plumbo supradicto. (*Liber Niger*, f. 80 *b*.)

The vague note of time, 'circa idem tempus,' is probably to be rendered definite by the following entry among the *recepta* in the abbot's treasurer's account for 1378—9: 'Et de iiij^{xx}li de officio sacriste Westm' in xij charres plumbi.'

In the summary of treasurers' accounts (*Lib. Nig.* f. 145 f.) we are told that in 1383—4 John Lakyngheth received £200 from the internal treasurer for doing certain matters to the profit of the church. Probably this is the reason why the treasury was empty.

E.

The Lease to the Widowed Queen.

This eindenture made bitwene John by the sufferaunce of god Abbot of the Monastery of seint Peter of Westm^{r} the Priour and covent of the same of the one partie And the most high and excellent Princesse Elizabeth by the grace of god Quene of England late wyf to the moost mighty Prince of famous memore Edward the iiijth late Kyng of Englond and of Fraunce and lord of Irelond on the other partie Witnesseth that the forsaid Abbot Priour and Covent consideryng and wele remembryng that the forsaid excellent and noble pryncesse in the tyme of her said late husbond our alder liege lord was unto the said Monastery verry especiall good lord aswele in protectyng and defendyng the libertes & ffrauncheses of the same as in bountevous and largely departyng of her goods to the edifying and reparacions of the ffabrice of the said monastery by the hole assent concent & will of all the Captre have graunted dimised and to ferme letyn unto the forsaid Quene a mansion with in the said Abbey called Cheynegatis Apperteynyng unto the Abbot of the said place for the tyme beyng with all the Howses Chambers Aisiaments and other Appertenaunces therunto belongyng To have and hold the forsaid mansion with Thappertenaunces and other premisses to the said Quene from the fest of Ester last passed before the date herof unto thende of the terme of xl yeres then next folowyng and fully to be complete Yeldyng therfor yerely to the same Abbot or his successor or theire Assignes x[li] of lawfull money of Englond duryng the said terme to be paid atte festis of Mighelmas and Ester by even porcions And the forsaid Quene at her propre costis and Charge shall sufficiently repaire uphold and mayntene the said mansion and voide clense repaire and make the gutter goyng from the kechen of the same as often as shall be necessary and behovefull And atte ende of her terme the said mansion with Thappertenaunces sufficiently repaired mayntened and upholden yeld up unto the forsaid Abbot Priour and Covent and theire Successours Also it is covenanted and agreed bitwne the parties abovesaid that the said Quene shall in no wise sell lete to ferme nor aliene her said yeres nor eny parte therof in the said mansion with Thappertenaunces to any other person or persones duryng the said terme And the Abbot Priour and Covent and their successours forsaid the said mansion with thappertenaunces to the said Quene in the manner and fourme aboverehersed shall warant ayenst all people by these presents Provided alwayes that yf it shall happen the same Quene to dye within the said terme of xl yeres as god defend that then this present graunt and lees immediately after her decesse be voide and of no strengthe And over this it is covenanted and agreed that yf it happen the said Rent to be behynd unpaid after any terme of the termes abovelymytted in party or in all that is to say the Rent of Mighelmasse terme at seint Martyns day in wynter then next folowyng and the Rent of Ester at Whitsontyde then next ensuyng that then it shalbe leefull to the said Abbot and his Successours in the forsaid mansion with the Appertenaunces to reentre And the said Quene therfrom to expelle and put out this lees and dimyssyon notwithstanding In Witnesse &c Yeven the x day of Juyll the yere of our lord god mcccclxxxvi And the first yere of the reigne of kyng Henry the vii[th]. (*Register* I. f. 4.)

F.

The Grant to Bishop Thirlby.

Henricus octavus....Sciatis quod nos de gracia nostra speciali ac ex certa sciencia et mero motu nostris dedimus et concessimus...reverendo in Christo patre Thome episcopo Westm' et successoribus suis episcopis Westm' imperpetuum totum scitum et ambitum domus mansionis et habitacionis communiter vocat' Cheynygates in Westm' in comitatu nostro Midd' in qua Willelmus nuper abbas nuper monasterii de Westm' inhabitavit unacum omnibus edificiis domibus terris et solo infra dictum scitum et ambitum existen' cum gardinis et ortis illi adjacen' in quo quidem scitu sive ambitu sunt quedam turris situat' et existen' ad introitum dicte habitacionis que quidem turris continet in longitudine a capite orient' abbuttant' super claustrum dicti nuper monasterii usque ad caput occiden' abbuttant' super le Elmes per estimacionem sexaginta et septem pedes et in latitudine capitis occiden' a parte boriali usque ad partem australem per estimacionem viginti quatuor pedes et duos polices et alia edificia et domus cum gardinis et solo adjacen' continen' per estimacionem a turr' predicta usque ad ecclesiam dicti nuper monasterii in latitudine capitis orien' abbuttant' super claustrum dicti nuper monasterii centum viginti et quatuor pedes et in latitudine capitis occident' abbuttant' versus domum pauperum vocat' the kynges almoshouse centum sexaginta et decem pedes ac in longitudine partis borialis abbuttant' super ecclesiam dicti nuper monasterii et super stratam regiam vocat' the Brode Sentwarye ducentas quinquaginta et octo pedes et in parte australi abbuttan' super lez Elmes ducentas triginta et novem pedes. Ac eciam damus et concedimus prefato episcopo et successoribus suis imperpetuum quartam partem tocius magni claustri dicti nuper monasterii cum edificiis scituat' et existen. super eadem que quidem quarta pars contigue et proxime adjacet eidem domui mansioni et habitacioni in Westm' predict' ac omnia illa edificia et domos vocat' le Calbege et le Blackestole ibidem que continet in longitudine a capite boriali abbutt' super predict' turr' usque ad caput australe abbutt' super turr' vocat' le Blackestole Towour per estimacionem quaterviginti et octo pedes ac omnia edificia terr' et sol' existen' inter predicta edificia vocat' le Calbege et le Blackestole ex parte occiden' et edificia et domos vocat' le ffrayter misericorde et magnam coquinam conventualem voc' le greate covent kechen dicti nuper monasterii ex parte orient" Damus eciam et per presentes concedimus prefato episcopo magnam illam aliam turrim lapidiam in Westm' predict' situat' et existen' in quodam loco vulgariter vocat' the Oxehalle ac eciam magnum orreum situat' et existen' in predicto loco vocat' the Oxehalle et domos et edificia illa existen' et situat' ibidem inter magnam fossam vocat' the Mylldam ex parte australi et predictum orreum ex parte boriali ac omnia alia edificia domos ortos terr' et solum ibidem situat' jacen' et existen' inter dictum orreum et inter dictos domos et edificia ex parte occiden' et predict' magnam turrim et domum vocat' the longe Granery ex parte orient' ac inter edificia et domos vocat' the Brewhouse and the Backehouse dicti nuper monasterii ex parte boriali et pred' magnam fossam vocat' the Mildam ex parte australi.

(Extract from *Munim.* Royal Charters, x. 1 : dated 20 Jan. 1541.)

By this charter there is granted to the bishop the whole site of the mansion called *Cheynygates* in Westminster in which the late abbot dwelt: namely

1. The tower at the entrance of the said dwelling, measuring in length, from the end next the cloister to the end next the Elms, 67 ft.; and in breadth at the western end 24 ft. 2 in.

2. The main site of the house and gardens; measuring on the east, along the cloister wall from the tower above-mentioned to the church, 124 ft.: on the west, 'abutting towards the King's Almshouse,' 170 ft.: on the north, first along the church and then along the Broad Sanctuary, 258 ft.: on the south, next the Elms, 239 ft.

The bishop's grant further includes

3. A fourth part of the cloister, with the buildings over the same: that is to say, the west walk next to his house.

4. The Calbege and Black Stole, measuring from the north, next the tower above mentioned, to the south, up to but not including the Black Stole Tower, 88 ft.

5. The site and buildings lying between these on the west and 'le Frayter Misericorde' and the great convent kitchen on the east. [It is possible to read 'le Frayter, Misericorde,' as separate terms.]

6. The other great stone tower in the place called 'the Oxehall'; and the great barn in the Oxehall; and the buildings there situate between the great ditch called the Mill-dam on the south and the barn on the north; and all else between these buildings on the west and the aforesaid great tower and the Long Granary on the east, and between the brewhouse and bakehouse on the north and the Mill-dam on the south.

A few preliminary remarks may be made on these various portions of the grant:

1. The effect of this tower which rises over the entrance to the cloister has been somewhat destroyed by the building of another storey to the adjoining house on the south. The length measurement is that of the two rooms over the entrance to the cloisters. 'The Elms' is a description of a portion of the present Dean's Yard, and is frequently met with in leases from the time of Henry VII.

2. This is apparently the extent of Abbot Litlyngton's site. The King's Almshouse was founded by Henry VII: the King's Almsmen survive, but are no longer housed within the precincts.

3. The cloister was at that time glazed, and the bishop could enter this walk privately from the N.E. corner of his garden. Nothing marks more pathetically the close of the monastic life. This was the first thing Lord Wentworth was called upon to restore; for when the old services were resumed in 1553, it was needed for the Sunday procession even before the monks came back.

4. The names 'Calbege' and 'Black Stole' have not been explained, but the buildings referred to are the houses now inhabited by a minor canon and by the archdeacon on the east side of Dean's Yard. One copy of the grant has 'Blackescole,' and Lord Wentworth's surrender has 'Black Schole.' But this is a mere misreading for we have much earlier evidence on the other side.

5. The space here granted is narrow; but the description is important for us, as it helps to indicate the position of the Misericorde.

6. These indications are most valuable for the topography of what is now Dean's Yard. The Long Granary, which was not given to the bishop, survived till the eighteenth century as the dormitory of the King's scholars.

I now add some explanatory notes, which with the further aid of the large Plan (in cover) will I hope suffice to illustrate the grant made to the bishop, and may also help to solve some outstanding problems.

1. CHEYNYGATES.

1300, 'Item j ser' cum iij clau' empt' ad host' de chaines. xijd.' Cellarer (J. Redyng) 1299—1300 (*Munim.* 18,830).

1486, 'a mansion within the said abbey called Cheynegatis.' Lease to Queen Elizabeth Wydville, printed above.

1539, To Hendon and Cheynygates for my lord. Subsexton's roll (*Munim.* 19,834).

c. 1540, 'the kechyn wythin Cheyngates': 'In the Warderobe at Cheneygates.' Dissolution Inventory, printed below.

1541, 'totum scitum et ambitum domus mansionis et habitacionis communiter vocat' Cheynygates.' Grant to Bp Thirlby, printed above.

2. CAWAGIUM.

1300, 'j ser' cum clau' ad cauag' pro tall' seruand'. iiijd.' Cellarer's roll (*Munim.* 18,830), under heading of granary and malthouse.

1387, entertainment of servants of the king 'in Cawag'.' Treasurers' roll.

1389, Plaster of Paris 'pro pariete noui cauag' plastrandi'; 1390, 'fenestr' in cauag''; 1392, Wall 'in cauag' Celar' dauband' et plastrand' cum plastro paris.' Cellarer's rolls.

1391 (after building of new celarium), 'circa domum supra novum cellerar' et cawagium'; 1397, repairs of Cawagium, &c.; 'pro host' et celar' Kawagii in pistrina.' Treasurers' rolls.

It is plain from these references that there was more than one Cawagium, and that the cellarer's Cawagium was an apartment connected with his business, as was the Blackstole. Probably it was over the cellarer's undercroft, and perhaps used for keeping his tallies. The Black Stool may have been where he sat to take his receipts and cast his accounts.

The mention of the 'Calbege' and the 'Blackstole' in Bishop Thirlby's grant suggests that they were above the undercroft which runs between the present porter's lodge and the headmaster's house. I think we may identify 'Calbege' with 'Cawagium.'

3. BLACKESTOLE.

1332, 'apud le Blakestol'' (some expenditure crossed out). Cellarer's roll (*Munim.* 18,831).

1372, 'Et pro factura le Blakestol in Celar' xiijs. iiijd.' Cellarer's roll.

1452, 'apud le Blackestole' (some payments received). So-called 'Prior's Rent Book' (exhibited in Chapter House) p. 61.

4. OXEHALL.

1532, 'reparacions done upon the faggot house in the Oxehall.' *Munim.* 24,860; cf. 24,854 (same year, 1531—2).

1541, 'turrim lapidiam...in quodam loco vulgariter vocat' the Oxehalle.' Grant to Bp Thirlby.

[In the Cellarer's roll, 1377—8: 'et in tribulis emp' pro domo boum. xiijd.']

5. THE KING'S ALMSHOUSE is mentioned in the grant to Bishop Thirlby as part of the western boundary of the mansion of Chenygates. It was built by King Henry VII for thirteen poor men, and was situate, as Stow tells us, on the south side of the great Gatehouse[1]. Its position is roughly indicated on Morden and Lea's plan of 1690, a reference to which I owe to the kindness of Mr Walter Spiers: but the words of the grant to Richard Cicill, quoted below, shew that the garden of the keeper of the Gatehouse was its northern boundary, and the plan does not shew the Gatehouse at all.

Among the Westminster Muniments are several interesting documents relating to this Almshouse.

(1) *Munim.* 5398 A and B: Covenants and specifications for its erection according to a *Plat* (which unfortunately is not forthcoming). The building was to be of brick, 120 ft. long and 26 ft. wide, with gable ends and tiled roof. The cost was to be £500. The signatories are Sir Richard Guldeford and Sir Thomas Lovell. The specifications give the number of bricks and of tiles to be employed.

(2) *Munim.* 5390: Bond from Nicholas Brigham Gentl. of Westminster to David Vincent, Armiger, in £40, for the making of a conduit at the Bedehouse for the use of the Almsmen; 30 Nov. 1547: signed by N. B.

(3) *Munim.* 5325 (undated): Petition of the King's Almsmen. They had been dispossessed by 'one David Vincent, being then an officer belonging to the wardrobb of beddes to the most worthie prince of famous memorie King Henry the viiith.' He afterwards 'sold the same unto one Nicolas Brigham, who converted the same to a dwelling house for hym selfe and to his use and took awaye the armes standing and fixed over the gate thereof.' There was a Hall and Chapel, as well as 'a severalle chamber' for each almsman. In the first year of Queen Elizabeth a commission of enquiry had been directed to the Dean and

[1] Stow's *Survey*, ed. Kingsford, II. 122.

Chapter as to this encroachment, and the almsmen complain to the Queen that they are still dispossessed.

Nicholas Brigham, who erected Chaucer's monument, died in Dec. 1558: see *Dict. of Nat. Biography.*

(4) *Munim.* 5321 (early seventeenth cent. hand):

The howse or Almeshouse which was graunted to Richard Cicell did belong [did belong] to the Abbot of Westm': which Abbey of Westm' was surrendered to king Hen: 8. in the xxxjth yere of his Raigne.

Aug. 5. Afterwards the said king Henry did errecte the Deane and Chapter of Westm' 34th yere of his Raigne. And did give and graunte to the said Deane and Chapter (among other landes) the said howse.

July 24. In the 38 yere of his Raigne the said Deane and Chapter by deede did graunt backe the said house to the king his heires and successours for ever afterwards king Edward the 6th by letters Pattents dated the xxxth of June in the first yere of his Rayne did give and graunt the said howse to Richard Cicell Esq. his heires and successours for ever.

The Recordes wherof you may find in the office
of the Court of Augmentations
And also the particulars and boundaries of the said howse.

(5) *Munim.* 5397: Commissioners under King James I in 1604 restore the Chapel, Hall and Kitchen, which had been alienated 2 Edw. VI and were in possession of Dame English under Lord Petre.

I am indebted to the courtesy of Mr E. G. Atkinson of the Record Office for the following transcript of the Record referred to in No. 4.

Records of the Court of Augmentations. Particulars for Grants,
38 Henry VIII.

Richard Cicill, grantee.

Parcelł possess̃ nuper pertineñ Eccł̃ie Cathedrali Westm̃ modo in mañ Dñi Regis per Decanum ⁊ Capit̃lm ib̃m dat̃ concess̃ ⁊ sursumreddit̃.

Domus voc̃ the Almeshouse scituat̃ infra precinctum nuper monasterii Westm̃ valet in

Exit̃ ⁊ proficuis totius illius partis domus Elimozinarie predc̃e vocat̃ le Almeshowse cũ pertineñ jaceñ ⁊ existeñ infra precinctum nuper monasterii Westmonasterii quondam edificat̃ per serenissimum Principem nuper Regem Henricum septimum scitt. Halle coquine cum le larder ⁊ laundrie ac le Buttrie unacum om̃ibz cameris desuper edificat̃ accum capella ⁊ gardino ac om̃ibz aliis parvis curtilag̃ ⁊ lez yardes eid̃m le Almeshouse ⁊ gardino adjaceñ prout insimul scituat̃ ⁊ jacent̃ inter c̃oem stratum duceñ versus dc̃m nuper monasterium Westm̃ ex parte orieñ ⁊ le Alley ib̃m adjaceñ juxta Edificia vocat̃ le poore menslodgynges ex parte occideñ unde capud australe abbuttat super stratum ib̃m ⁊ capud boriale inde abbuttat super gardinum modo vel nuper Alex̃i Palmer custodis Prisone vocat̃ le Gatehowse in Westm̃ et que continent in longitud̃ ex parte orieñ lxxix pedes ꝛ d̃i ꝛ ex parte occideñ iiij^xx^xv pedes ꝛ capud australe continet in latitud̃ iiij^xx^vj pedes ꝛ capud boriale continet in latitud̃ lxv pedes sic nuperime superius per officiar̃ Dñi Regis nunc ꝛ arentat̃ cõibz annis per annum ad xxxix^s^. v^d^. ob̃.

Concordat cum valore fact̃ per decanum ꝛ capitl̃m eccl̃ie cath̃ie predc̃e tempore concessionis premissoꝝ dño Regi per eosdem decanum ꝛ capitl̃m per me

Ric̃m Duke.

6. Bakehouse and Brewhouse.

Munim. 35,762: Lease of Bakehouse, etc. by Abbot [Feckenham], etc. 8 Dec. 1558.

To Ralph Petrie of the same house Baker...have demised...all that their ten^t^ commonlie called the bakehouse with the next lodging to the same on the west end Set lyeing and being on the west syde of the said mon' within the Abbey with the two ovens in the said bakehouse with all and singuler thappertenances: which said backhouse and lodging containe in length from theast to the west lxxxvi foote of Assise and on breadth from the north to the south xviii foote of Assyse. And the ii ovens stretching xiii foote deepe into the millhouse on the southside of the said bakhouse conteine in breadth east to west xxiii foote [Also one yard or voyd ground on the south side of the said bakhouse lying betwyxt the petycannons lodging and the Diche that serveth the houses of office to the said mon' belonging conteyning from the east to the west and from the north to the south equally xl foote of a size].

The words in brackets are struck out; clearly because this ground was to be let to the brewer with the brewhouse.

Munim. 35,769: Lease of Brewhouse, etc. by Abbot [Feckenham], etc. 2 Jan. 1559.

To William Porter...in consideracion of a certen somme of money to them towards the charges of the newe bylding of their commen Bruehouse beforehand paid...have demised...all that their teniment commonlie called the bruehouse and a myllhouse and a lyme kell adioining to the same on the west ende: bounding on the Grammar schole eastward And the newe byldings called the peticannons lodgings on the west With a plot of ground adnexed to the west ende of the mill-house conteyning in length westwards to the henhouse ende lv foote and from thence to the dyche Southward fortie foote Also...the great Towr standing betwixt the said bruehouse and the Long garner, The bruehouse on the north the garner on the south; with all and singler the Romes and chambers into the said Tower and unto the same belonging and now appertaining above and beneath with a piece of the storehouse under the garner of length xlii foote and of breadth xxxiii foote adioyning to the lowest rome of the said Tower southward Set lyeing and being all together within the Abbey of Westm^r aforesaid.

[Attached is the inventory of vessels and implements in the brewhouse and millhouse.]

G.

Dissolution Inventories.

Public Record Office, Land Revenue, Miscellaneous Books, vol. 110: *Inventories of the Monastery of S. Peter, Westminster*[1].

An Inuentorye of the Butterye Remaynynge in the custodye of Gabriell Palley, to thuse of the late Abbotte.

Examinatur

Plate rem*ayn*-*yng* there ij basones & ij Ewers data Decano

In primis ij basons & iij ewers of syluer percell gylte eyther of the Basons hauynge A man in a tre Slepinge[2] & everye of the Ewers haiuynge Islyppe in the printe of the Cover*e*.

a bason & one Ewer of syluer white deliberantur Thesaurario ad vsum Regis ponderis—iiij^xx ij oz.

Examinatur

Item a lesser bason of syluer percell gylte wyth saint Edwardys armes in the printe of the bosse.

Examinatur
Dantur Decano

Item a grete standinge salte of syluer and gylte wythe a couer of the same hauunge droppys Rounde aboute the salte & couer.

Examinatur

Item a grete standinge salte of syluer and gylte wyth droppys all aboute hyt.

Examinatur
Dantur decano

Item ij lesser standinge salt*es* wyth on couer of Syluer and gylte viij square the knappe of the cover goinge of and on wyth a vise[3] and the lyppe of on square of the couer wantinge.

[1] The first part of these Inventories, relating to the church, is printed in the *Transactions of the London and Middlesex Archæological Society*, vol. IV, part iii (Aug. 1873) by the Reverend M. E. C. Walcott; but of the remainder he gave a few selected extracts only. They have now been copied for me in full by Miss E. M. Thompson (April—May, 1905). The smaller type of the side-notes and inserted words indicates the notes of the officials who checked and distributed the goods: words deleted by them are placed here in square brackets.

I have not attempted to explain all the curiosities and blunders of these interesting documents: but I have appended a few explanatory notes, partly from the Oxford English Dictionary; and I have given some of Mr Walcott's notes, placing his initials after them.

[2] 'A man in a tree slipping' is one of several forms of Abbot Islip's rebus: cf. p. 31, 'a man in a tree holding a slyppe': called simply 'Islypps,' p. 38.

[3] 'Screwing off and on,' as we should say. A 'vise' is the old name for a winding staircase.

Examinatur	Item a salte wythe owte a couer of syluer percell gylte viij square printyd wyth Rosys portculysis and crosse kayes[1].	Deliberatur Thesaurario ad vsum Regis *ponderis*— xiij oz.
Stollen	Item a drinkinge kuppe with a couer of syluer and gylte goblett ffassyon sett with skoloppe shell*is* bothe the couer and the kupp.	
Examinatur Datur Decano	Item a drinkinge cuppe wyth a cover of syluer and gylte nutte ffassyon wyth a hande holdinge a slyppe on the toppe of the cover.	
Examinatur Datur Decano	Item a kuppe of syluer and gylte hauinge ij erys and a cover of the same wyth a slyppe in the toppe of the cover wyth thys scrypture soli deo honor et gloria abougte the cuppe.	
Examinatur Datur Decano	Item a drinkinge Cuppe of syluer and gylte wyth ij erys and a cover of the same wrowghte a boute the Cuppe with Antykke worke.	
Examinatur one with the couer Dantur Decano [ij dantur Decano pro Rege]	Item iij drinkinge sortable Cuppes and on cover all of Syluer and gylte of chekar worke wth whyche Cuppes sume tyme apperteynid vnto the selerer[2] and were vsyd for swete wynes.	ij Cuppis withoute couers deliberantur ad vsum Regis Thesaurario ponderis— xiij oz. d̄i.
Examinatur	Item a lytell drinkinge Cuppe of syluer wyth on Ere, white.	deliberatur Thes*aurario* *ponderis*— v. oz. d̄.
Examinatur m^um the couer lackyth	Item a standinge nutte *with* a foote garnisshyd and a couer all of syluer & gylte hauyng a man in a tre holdinge a slyppe in the toppe of the couer and wrytten a boute the nutte Da gloriam deo.	Deliberatur Thesaurario
Examinatur Datur Decano	Item a chafyndysshe of Sylver & gylte.	
Examinatur	Item a grete standinge nutte wyth a fote garnysshed & a cover all of syluer and gylte hauinge ane Acorn in the toppe.	Deliberatur Thesaurario
Examinantur xviij dantur decano	Item x syluer sponys every on of them hauinge an apple on the ende and touchyd wythein.	
Examinatur	Item on syluer spone wyth God and the worlede in hys hande of syluer and gylte at thende and towchyd wythin.	vij white deliberantur Thesaurario ponderis— vij oz.
Examinantur	Item iij syluer sponys every of them hauinge the apple of Syluer and gylte at thende and vn towchyd wythin.	
Examinantur	Item vij Syluer Sponys every on of them hauynge a woodwarde[3] of Syluer and gylte at thende.	
Examinatur	Item iiij Syluer Sponys every on of them hauinge a lyon of Syluer and gylte at thende.	

[1] So below, p. 35, 'peter Kayes': the arms of the abbey. [2] *i.e.* the Cellarer.

[3] 'Woodward, a keeper who looks after woods. Woodwose, a wild man.' M. E. C. W.

Examinatur

Item a greate Syluer spone and gylte wyth a flatte knappe on thende and towchyd wythin.

pro Decano

Item ij brode karvinge knyves and a brekinge[1] knyffe Sortable beinge sume what olde hauynge haftys of Iverye and barryd wyth syluer and gylte.

Pro Decano

Bvtterye knyves

Item ij meate knyfes for my lorde hys trencher wyth on botkin[2] belonginge to the same (beinge haftyd wyth dogyn and at thendys of the same haftys beinge stoppyd wyth syluer a pon the shethe a Chape[3] of sylver.

Pro decano

Item a standynge case of smalle meate knyfes or trencher knyfes lakkinge there of v. knyves and Remaynynge in the same case xxij Knyfe the Sheve therof havinge ij barrys of sylver about hytte.

pro decano

Item a stokke of trencher knyfes wyth Iron haftys whych my lorde hadd lorde Hussey conteynyng xij knyves[4].

Naperye warre of Dyaper.

Table clothes of Dyaper totum pro decano

Item the beste table clothe conteynynge in lenght xiij yardys and di*midium* in bredeth ij yardys and di*midium*.

Item an other table cloth cont*eynynge* in lengh viij yard*is* and iij qu*arters* In bredeth ij yardys and a quarter.

Item a table clothe cont*eynynge* in length iiij yardys and a quarter. In Breade ij yardys and a quarter.

Item a table clothe cont*eynynge* iiij yardys iij quarter and more and in bread on yarde and di*midium*.

Item an other table clothe cont*eynyng* in lengh iiij yardys In Breade on yarde di*midium*.

Item an other table cloth conteynyng in lenghth vij yard*is* quarter and in bredeth ij yardys quarter.

Item a other table clothe cont*eynyng* in breade ij yardys skante in length ix yardis.

Item an other table cloth cont*eynyng* in length vij yardys and more and in bredeth ij yardis quarter et di*midium* q*uarteri*.

Item an other table clothe cont*eynyng* in length v. yardis d*imidium* and in bredethe a yarde quarter di*midii*.

Longe Towels of Dyaper totum pro decano

Item a Towell of Dyaper cont*eynyng* in lenghthe xv yardys In brede on yarde.

Item an other towell cont*eynyng* in lengthe xiiij yard*ys* quarter and in breade iij quarters.

[1] 'Carving: to break was to cut up a deer. Hall speaks of carving and breaking meat.' M. E. C. W.

[2] *i.e.* with one bodkin, or small dagger.

[3] The mounting at the point of the sheath.

[4] See 'Hussey, Sir John, Baron Hussey,' *Dict. Nat. Biogr.* 'On 15 May [1537] he was tried with Lord Darcy at Westminster...and sentenced to be executed at Tyburn.'

Item an other towell conteynyng in lengthe x yardys iij quarters and In brede iij quarters.

Item an other towell conteynyng iiij yardis di*midium* in brede iij q*uarters*.

Item an other towell conteynyng viij yardys and in brede iij q*uarters*.

Item an other towell co*nteynyng* iiij yardys quarter and in brede iij quarters.

Item an other towell cont*eynyng* viij yardis quarter and in brede iij q*uarters*.

Hande Towells of Dyaper

Item the Fynest hande Towell conteynyng in lenghth ij yardys di*midium et* dimidium quarteri and in bredeth on yarde and q*uarter*. totum pro Decano

Item iij hande Towells conteynyng in lenghthe everye of them ij yardys dimidium and in brede iij q*uarters*.

Item an other hande Towell conteynyng in leghthe iij yardys iij quarters in bredeth d*imidium* yarde.

Cubberde clothe of Dyaper

Item a cubberde clothe conteynynge in lenghthe iij yardys & in breadhth ij yardys and a q*uarter*.

A coverpane of Dyaper

Item a Fyne coverpane cont*eynyng* in lenghth one yarde and quarter and in bredeth iij quarters.

Dyaper Napkins

Item vj fyne Napkins of damaske worke newe And vj other dyaper Napkins sore worne.

Table clothes of playne clothe

Item a Fyne table cloth cont*eynyng* in lenghth vj yardys d*imidium* and in bredeth on yarde and q*uarter*.

Item a Table clothe cont*eynyng* in length iij yardys iij quarters and in bredeth on ell.

Playne Towells

Item a Fyne playne Towell conteynyng v. yardys and a quarter. Item a playne Towell cont*eynyng* in lenghth iij yardys di*midium*.

Item a Towell cont*eynyng* in length iij yardys and in brede iij qu*arters*.

Item an olde playne Towell.

Necke Towells

Item iij necketowells every of them cont*eynyng* in lenghth a yarde iij quarters and in bredeth dimidium yarde.

Item an other necke towell conteynynge ii yard*is*, in brede di*midium*.

Item an other necke towell cont*eynyng* on yard iij quarters.

Item an other necke towell cont*eynyng* iij yardys iij quarters.

Cubbarde Clothes

Item fyve Cubberde Clothes everye of them cont*eynyng* in lenghth on yarde thre quarter and in bredeth a yard and a quarter.

Item a playne Cubberde clothe.

Napkyns

Item xxv. playne Napkyns.
Item xviij fyne playne Table napkins.
Item xviij playne Course napkins.

Item vj olde noughty Napkins for the dryinge of plate.
Item vj Newe dyaper napkins.
Item iij dossen of playn napkins newe.

Fyne Trenchers — Item a case of fyne trenchers for frute wyth a doss*en* trenchers off pewter of the newe Fassyon.

Butterye Stuffe remaynynge in the Charge of Edmunde Vincent.

In the charge of Edmonde Vyncent — Item iij pewter basons and on Ewer. — totum pro Decano
Item iij buttery knyves.
Item xiiij lethern Gyspyns[1].
Item a Kandelstykke of latten with ij nosys and ij flowers.
Item a greate bell candelstykke w*i*th a nose to put on.
Item a greate kandelstycke bell fassyon with a flower.
Item iij grete candelstyck*is* of on sorte w*i*th flowers.
Item on kandylstykke of lumbard Fassyon[2].
Item on lyttell bell Candelstykke with a flowre.
Item vj bell candelstykk*is* sortable with flowers.
Item v. bell candylstykk*is* of a lesse sorte w*ith*owt flowers.
Item the Fyer panne perteynynge to the hall.
Item iiij newe Table Clothes playn*e* for the hall.
Item a cobberd clothe playn in lenghth on yard di*midium*.
Item vj newe Table clothes of canvas for the hall.
Item iij playn clothes very shorte.

Plate and Implement*is* of Housolde Remaynynge in the Mysericorde.

Examinatur — In primis a Salte of Syluer and gylte wyth A cover Full of droppes po*nderis*— xxxj oz. — Examinatur Deliberantur Thesaurario

Examinatur — Item iiij Salt*is* of Syluer wyth Rosys and perculysys [pcell gylte] po*nderis*— lj oz. (white) — Examinatur

Examinatur Datur Decano — Item a standynge pece w*i*th a cover gylt to drinke wyne in. po*nderis* xxij oz.

Examinantur — Item ij Syluer pecys on bygger then the other and iiij other Syluer pecys of byggenesse po*nderis*— lxix oz. [lxij oz.] — d*eliber*atur Thes*aurario*

Examinantur — Item ij Syluer pott*is* on wyth a handyll and the other wyth owte po*nderis*— xij oz. [xiiij oz.] (white) — Deliberatur Thesaurario

[1] Gispin, a leathern pot or cup, 'One of the said watch to fetch a pott and a gespin att the Pitcherhouse for ale and wyne (Ordin. for the household, 347).' M. E. C. W.

[2] 'j tabula depicta ad modum Lumbard, 22 Edw. III. iij tabule de opere Lumbardorum (Inv. Edw. III). j imago de cupro voc' Lumbard pertere, 25 Edw. III (MS. Add. 24, 525, fo. 261).' M. E. C. W.

Item iij Masers *with* owte bossys and with bossys xiij. — deliberantur Thesaurario

Examinantur — ij geven to the Deane

white
Item ix Syluer Sponys *ponderis*— viij oz. — deliberantur Thesaurario
vij *ponderis*—vj oz. et di*midium*

Examinatur

Item an other Salte of Sylver percell gylte wyth a Cover *with* Rosys perculysys and peter Kayes *ponderis*— xxij oz. — Examinatur Deliberatur Thesaurario

Examinantur

white
Item iiij other Saltys of Syluer *ponderis*— xlj oz. — Examinantur deliberantur Thesaurario

mum ther lackyth ij Spones

white
Item xxiiij sylver Sponys *ponderis*— xxv oz. — xxij deliberantur Thesaurario, ponderis— xxiij oz.

Examinatur

Item xix masers on of them wyth owt a bosse *ponderis*. — Deliberantur Thesaurario

Item a blacke nutte wyth a cover the fote garnysshyd wyth Syluer, *ponderis* wyth the nutte xxij oz. — deliberantur Thesaurario

The Naperye.

In primis A dyaper table cloth with a payer of touels of Dyaper very olde.

Item iiij table clothys wherof ij be olde and ij payer of towells.

Item iiij Napkyns and a hande towell.

Item v. Basons wyth ewers of pewter.

Item vj Candelstykk*is* on of them wyth ij nosys.

Item a payer of Andorns a payer of tong*is* and a colerake A chafer A tosting Iron and A Frying pan.

Item vj cusshyns of olde tappestrye.

Item xxiij platters vij dysshes and vj sawcers.

Item a brasse potte and an olde Kettell.

Item a saint Johnes hed of wood[1].

The Inuentorye of the kechyn wythin Cheyngate[2].

remanent — Brasse pottes — Dantur Decano except*is* ut infra

In primis a boyling pan bounde wyth Iron.

Item a Brasse potte wyth an Iron bayle.

Item an other brasse potte wyth an Iron bayle.

Item An other lyttell brasse potte of Bulleyn Mettell, And a lyttell newe brasse pott cont*eynyng* ij Gallons and more.

[1] 'A representation of the Decollated Head of the Baptist. A Seynt Johns hede of Alabaster (Bury Wills, 115, 116). There is one at St John's Hospital, Winchester.' M. E. C. W.

[2] For the name Cheynygates, see above, p. 26.

[mum the greate panne remayneth] Brassepannys

Item A grete newe pan cont*eynyng* xl^{ti} gallons And a pan of x gallons And ij pannys on bounde on of them cont*eynyng* v gallons and the other iiij gallons.

Item a pan of Red mettell cont*eynyng* iiij Gallons. Item a pan bonde wyth Iron wyth ij handels cont*eynyng* vj gallons. Item a brasse pan vnbounde cont*eynyng* iiij gallons. Item an other brasse pan con-*teynyng* v. gallons. Item a pan wyth ij yron handels cont*eynyng* iiij Gallons. Item a lyttle pan vnbounde conteynynge on gallon. Item an other pan cont*eynyng* iij gallons. Item a walter Tanker[1] bounde wyth Irons. Item a lyttell newe skylles wyth iij fete and a hande of Iron.

latten

Item a cullender of brasse. Item a brasyn ladell. Item a brasen Skymer*e* the handell of Iron. Item A brasyn morter wyth an Iron pestell. Item chafyndysshys. Item a Fylling ladle with an Iron Sokett.

Chafers of bullen

Item a ij handed chaffer wyth iij fete cont*eynyng* by estymacyon iiij gallons. Item a lyttell chaffer wyth iij feete and a handell con-*teynyng* a pottell. Item a standynge chafer to set in the Fyer wyth on handell. Item a goodlye grete chafer havinge iij feete and ij handels. Item a lesser chaffer havinge iij fete and ij handels.

Iron ware

Item iij grete Iron Rakkys ij of them sortable ye other of a lesser sorte. Item on gredyron. Item a gredyron of xij barrys. Item a fyre Shulve. Item a Iron peele[2]. Item an olde Fryinge pan wyth a broken start. Item ij other frying panns on bygger then An other. Item iij drepinge pann*is* of Iron. Item a grete tryvet. Item a lyttell tryvet. Item a befe prykke. Item ij hokis callyd potte hokys. Item a Fryinge Slyse of Iron.

Spytt*is*

Item ij grete Iron spytt*is* square. Item a longe byrde broche square. Item iij grete Iron spytt*is* Rounde. Item a lesser Rounde byrde broche.

Knyves For the Kychyn

Item a grete course. Item a strykinge knyffe al of Iron. Item a mynsing Knyfe. Item iij Choppinge knyves. Item a wood Axe.

One Stone morter and a stone trough remayneth

Kychyn Stuffe

Item iij grete stone morters. Item a lesser stone morter wyth iij wood pestell*is*. Item a grete bred grate. Item vj. flaskett*is*. Item vij woodden trees. Item iiij wooddon bolles. Item ij grete boxes on for otemell and the other for salte. Item ij watter skeppes. Item ij lyttell barrels for verges and veneger. Item the kychyn colleke[3] of lether. Item ij grete beringe tubbes[4]. Item a powderinge tubbe wyth a cover iij bryne tubbes and a sowsinge tubbe. A lyttell stonding borde iij emptye Runlett*is* ij drye hoggesheddes. A drye tubbe iiij close baskett*is* of wykers and ij wyth owte covers. Item ij hoggesheddys for salt a grete cheste for otemele. Item a hoggeshedde wyth varges.

[1] Probably a water tank. [2] A shovel. [3] 'Colette (pail).' M. E. C. W.

[4] Perhaps herring tubs.

Pewter — Item iij chargers. Item xlviij platters xlviij dyshes and xlj sausers all of the sylver fassyon.

Cesterns *remayn* — Item ij cesternes of leade.

An Inuentory of the Housold stuffe.

In Mr Thyxtyls Chamber. In custodia do*mini* Epis*copi* excepto le bedested in ma*nibus* Decani et id*em* in custo*dia* d*icti* Epi*scopi* ad vsum R*egis* — In primis a fetherbed with iij blewe gardys[1] at eyther ende. A bolster a pyllowe wyth a bere of lokeram[2] A koverlet of tapstrye A grete standynge beddstede A payer of Andyrons A pyllowe of Downe coveryd wyth fustyan a grete spuse[3] cheste bounde wyth Iron and going of vj Iron whelys A course table a payer of trestels a playn chest wyth lokke and key a longe cofer.

In Mr Meltons Chamber — In primis a (rem*ayneth*) playne bedsted a grete Fetherbed a bolster ij pyllows of downe a bere of lokeram a matteresse stuffyd wyth wooll ij wollen blankettes j Iryshe blankett A large coverlet of blewe dornykys[4] a (rem*ayneth*) trokyll bedsted a newe fetherbedd wyth a newe edge aboute hyt a table wyth a sete lyke a cheyre An olde carpet of tapstrye worke a bedsted wyth a sealer[5] ij curteyns all of grene saye dowble fringede the Chamber hangyd complete wyth grene saye A lyttell boffet forme[6].

In Sulyard*is* Chamber — Item a lyttell fether bed a large bolster ij pyllowes of fustyan a feble coverlet of tapstrye very olde an nother newe coverlet. — Soluta Thesaurario

sold to John Masshe for iij^s. iiijd.

Mr Morres Chamber — Item a fetherbed an olde bolster a pyllowe an olde coverlet of tapstrye An Iryshe mantell a turned (rem*ayneth*) chayre | An olde table (rem*ayneth*) wyth folden leavys & other bordys.

In the gallorye[7] — In primis a hanginge of Redde and grene saye a staynyd cloth of Saynt George ij Carpett*is* in the wyndows of tapstrye worke | a lyttle table of quene Johans Armes[8]. — Dantur Decano

Jeru*salem* parlor — Item vij pecys of (rem*anent* cum Epi*scopo*) hanging*is* of Arres worke wyth ij lyttle pecys of Arras wyth the story of Planett*is* | A (sold to the Deane xjj s) wyndowe carpett wrought apon

[1] Ornamental borders or trimmings.

[2] Lockram is a linen fabric, named from Locronan in Brittany.

[3] Walcott suggests 'spruce wood.'

[4] A fabric named from Dornewich (Tournay).

[5] A tester (?), as below.

[6] A low stool or form.

[7] The order in which the Gallery, Jerusalem Chamber and Jericho Parlour are here given suggests that the Gallery beyond Jerusalem, which has now disappeared, is referred to: see above, p. 15.

[8] Perhaps Joan of Navarre, queen of Henry IV, who died in 1437.

sold to the Dean
pakethrede full of Redd Roses | And olde carpet For A wyndowe be-
for xij d. *remanet* cum
longing to the same parlour of turkye worke | An olde Bawdkyn[1] for
Ep*iscopo* sold to the Deane—v.s.
the baye wyndowe towardys the brode saintuarye | A table carpet of
rem*anent* cum Ep*iscopo* sold to
tapstery | ij quyssyns Coueryd wyth grene braunchyd velvet. v. carpet
the Deane for—v.s. rem*anet* cum Ep*iscopo* sold to the deane for ij.s.
quisshons A table wyth a payer of trestells | A grete longe foldinge
d*atur* Decano D*atur* Decano rem*anet* cum
table | An Oestre table foldinge[2] | A skryne wyth wykars | A standinge
Ep*iscopo* rem*anent* cum Ep*iscopo* sold to the
cubberde w*i*th ij Ambereyes[3] | ij Joyned formes A payer of Andyorns
Dean for v.s.
A fyre forke of Iron. [A flaunders Cheyre] xviij boffet stolys
of the whiche vj doth rem*ayne* w*ith* the bysshoppe and xij geven to the Deane.

In the entrie betwene the hall and the perlour

one rem*anet* cum Ep*iscopo* et al*ter* sold to the Deane
Item ij Cobbordys And on playn forme

In Jerico[4] parlor

sold to the Deane for— xx.d.
viijd. xvj.d ij.s.
Item a payer of trestells | a Flaunders cheyre ij Joynyd Formes vi
vijj.s. v.s.
quisshyons of carpet worke wyth Islypps | A payer of Andyrons A
xiij.s. iiij.d. vj.s. viii.d.
standing cubberde carvyd A carpett of brode grene cloth A newe
geven to the Deane
Joyned Cheyre wyth a stole in hyt.

r' Decanus
In my lordys newe Chappell[5]

Item ij pecys of tappestrye of the planett*is* ij wyndowe carpett*is* of Tente worke hauinge the grounde whyte and full of Redd hartys A quysshyon of tapstrye | A pece of Redde saye lynyd wyth canvas.

Examinantur
In the lyttle Chamber nexte

the couerlet
Item a fetherbed a large bolster a pyllowe a couerlet of tapstre
with the Deane rem*anent* cum Ep*iscopo*
wyth byrdes and flowers iij pecys of hangingis of Redd and grene saye.
geven to the Deane
A close bedstocke A presse wyth a kokke and levyd.

Examinantur[6]
The Halle

Item a grete olde Arres at the hye dease ij bankers of tapestrye ij hangingis for the syde of the hall of grene saye. A gret Joyned Chayre for the Quenys Coronacyon An olde grene banker the Arrasys in the Hall and in the parlour And a fest(i)ual in Printe[7]. remanent cum Ep*iscopo*

[1] A rich stuff: properly of gold and silk threads.

[2] 'A lytell oyster tabull (Wareham's Inv. C. $\frac{1}{18}$ P. R. O. fo. 23).' M. E. C. W.

[3] Aumbries, or cupboards (*armarii*).

[4] Walcott, writing in 1873, found it necessary to put the note, 'That ordinarily called now the Organ-room': but the older name is at the present time in exclusive possession.

[5] See the separate note on 'The Abbot's Chapel' (p. 84).

[6] From this point onwards the notes of examination are not here reproduced.

[7] We may suppose that this was one of Caxton's books, printed over the Gate leading to the Almonry. The Festival is thus described in the *Old Service-books of the English*

In the Skolyons Chamber	Item ij matteressys ij Canvas bolsters an olde coverlet a blanket and a bedsted.	appoynted to be geven to a pore man
In the Portors lodge	Item a bedsted and a lyttell Fetherbed full of blewe strykys A bolster an olde pyllow A blanket of Irysshe Frees An olde coverlet remanet cum Episcopo of tapestrey set wyth Flowers a standinge Cubbarde wyth an Ambery lokkyd.	geven to M[r] Deane
In Syr Radulph*is* Chamb*er*	Item a fetherbed a bolster ij pyllowys a pyllow bere a large coverlet of tapestrye wyth Imagys a wollen blanket hanging*is* for the Chamber rem*ayneth* rem*ayneth* of fullerye worke a stondyng bedd and a trokyll bedsted and an olde presse.	geven to M[r] Deane
In the lyttle chamber over the comon Jakys	Fetherbedde Item a boster a course pyllowe ij wolleyn blankett*is* A kelter coverlet of Flaunders makinge lately bought the hanging*is* complete about the chamber And a testor of Fullerye worke A bedsted and a forme.	geven to the Deane
m[m] the bedde in Adames Chamber moste deliuer-ed to this Chamber & thother to be receyued in the place of this.	Item a Fetherbed ij bolsters ij wolleyn blankettis Full of Hooles rem*ayneth* A cov*er*let of blewe and grene dornix lynyd wyth canvas A bedsted a rem*ayneth* lyttell Cubbard.	
In Tytleys Chamber		
In Gabriels chamber	Item a bedsted ij course cubberd*is* and ij lyttle formes.	rem*anent*
In the Wardrobe at Cheneygates	[Item an olde bedtester of blewe bokeram lynyd wyth canvas. Item a whytt quylt wyth a lambe brothered in the myddys. | Item a	geven to pore folk*is*

Church, by Wordsworth and Littlehales (1904), p. 142: 'A few months before he had finished his "Golden Legend" Caxton had issued, in June, 1483, another folio volume of somewhat similar character. It was an edition of the "Festial," "Festyval," or *Liber Festivalis*, which is ascribed to John Myrc, Austin Canon of Lilleshall, Salop, *cir.* 1420, author of "Instructions to Parish Priests," in English verse, taken from the *Pars Oculi*, ascribed either to W. de Pagula or to Wa. Paker, of Cornwall, and edited by Mr Peacock for E. E. Text Soc. in 1868.

'After a pious quatrain, the author of the *Festival* says:—

'"[By] Myn owne symple vnderstandynge I fele wel how it fareth by other that ben in the same degree and heven (*i.e.* "have") charge of soules, and holde to teche theyr paryshens of all the pryncypall festes *th*at come in the yere, shewyng vnto them what the holy sayntes suffred and dyde for goddes sake and for his loue."

'And because "many excuse theym for defaute of bookes, and also by symplenes of connynge. Therfore in helpe of suche clerkes this treates is drawen out of *Legenda Aurea*."......

'The "*Festyval*"... was printed at least fifteen times from 1483 to 1532.'

Redd sumpter cloth moche eaten wyth Ratt*is*.] Item an olde coverlet
sold to the Deane for ij.s. to geven to pore folk*is*
of tapsterye worke whyte and Red. Item ij olde matteresses. Item
to be geven to pore folk*is*
a boster [wyth whyte hartys] on canvas boster stuffyd wyth flokkis.
j at Belloys ij to be sold
Item iij pyllows. Item on old quysshyn wyth whyte hartys in the myddis. Item one quysshyne of tapstre wyth grypys in the mydd*is*. Item on olde pece of Redde clothe in lenghth ij yardys. Item on old grene quisshyn of tapstre wyth a grete Flower in the myddeste. [Item an olde grene quisshyn of tapstre wyth a Skechyn and Jħus in the myddys.] Item on olde quisshon of dornyx. Item an olde Qussyon of baudekyn. [Item iij lyttell pecys of lyttell bankers p... of tappestre.]
bokeram geven to Mr. Deane
Item other iij pecys of blewe [stayned cloth]. Item on large coverlet of tapestrye set wyth Imagerye and lynyd wyth canuas [Item a pece of caunvas ij yardys longe and ell brode.] Item on pece of grene saye wyth A border of v. yardys in length hanginge before the grete presse in the warderop. Item a tester of paintyd clothe wyth the coronacyon
sold to Mr. Deane for— xvj.d.
of owr lady in the mydd*is*. Item iiij payntyd clothes hanginge in the warderop. Item one olde coverlet of them that were laste bowgth.
remanent cum Episcopo
excepto vno. one geven to the Deane & thother re*mayneth* remanet
Item ij bedsted*is*. Item ij trokell bedsteddis in the grete close presse.
sold to the Deane for—v.s.
Item a grete cheste in the warderope. Item ij pyllow berys of lokeram. Item an olde pelow bere wyth a redd border of Sylke. Item an pece of olde stayned clothe. Item A cusshyon coveryd wyth whyte lether and
one rem*ayneth cum* Ep*iscopo* et alter
venditur decano v.s. geven to Mr
stuffyd wyth fethers ij bare hydes. Item an olde tyke fyllyd wyth
Deane remayneth
newe fethers. An olde presse open aboue. Item a fetherbed wyth a grete pece and a bolster to the same A large coverlet of tappestrye w*ith* Imagerye. Item ij payer of fyne flaxe shetys sume what olde. j flaxen shete of ij bredis dimidium. Item ij payer of canvas shetys sume what olde. Item on payer of large holand shetys in Master Meltons Chamber. Item ij payer of lokeram shetis and xviij payer of
geven [sold] to the deane [for—iij.*s*. iiij.*d*.]
canvas shetys. Item a Flaunders cheste standinge at the stayre foote going vp in to the warderop whych ys to ley shetys in. Item a fether bedde a coverlet and a bolster. Item a good fether bed a bolster a pyllowe of downe a grete large blankette mothe eton a coverlet of dornyx. A matteres on of them that was laste bowght and a bolster

[Left margin:] x fetherbedd*is* w*ith* bolsters pillowes couerlett*is* blankett*is* sold to the Deane with xxv^th^. payre of shetes for— xiii.li.vj.s. viijd.

m^um^ one payre of shetes in Thystell*is* chamber

[Right margin:] one payr geven to powr folkis one payre to Patche[1] and one to bery hym

geven to the Deane

[1] 'Patchys chamber' is mentioned just below. 'Patches house,' near the 'dark entry' and 'privy dorter,' is mentioned in the first Chapter Book (fo. 68, Jan. 1550; cf. fo. 74, 3 Dec. 1552). A John Pache was the abbey carpenter in 1446, and he was succeeded by Richard Pache: see Mr Rackham's 'Nave of Westminster' (*Brit. Acad, Proceedings*, IV, 24 *n*.).

very thykke stuffyd wyth fethers. Item a counter poynt the grounde very grene wyth flowers & roses. [Item a counter payn kelter couerlet whyche was won of them that wasse laste bought ij wollen blankettis on of them ys send to Henden as M[r]. Doctor sayth.] Item a Fetherbed well fylled wythe A tycke havinge blewe lystys and pesyd at the on syde An other fetherbed very olde. Item ij olde pyllowes of tykke and well stuffyd wyth Fethers. A large Matteres of Floxe yl stuffyd an olde matteres well stuffyd wyth Floxes ij lyttell olde matteresses in manner nothyng worthe An olde strall Item a newe strayll a payer of wollen blankettis A bolster of canuas stuffyd wyth fethers ij good fether beddis on hauing a pece in the myddes and ij bolsters wyth a pyllowe Item vij pecys arras sortable of Imagerye and lynyd wyth canuas.

(interlined: geven to Mr Deane; geven to pore folk; dat[r] decano) Dantur

Item iij pecis of Tapestry *with* a fetherbedd couerlett Teast*our* Shetis and blankett*is*.

In the Stable — Item a newe matteres whyche was on of the vj that was bought. A newe coverlett whyche was on of the vj that was laste bought A good smalle tycke bolster stuffyd wyth Fethers. — The Kyng*is* ser*uaunt* Portenary hath the Stuff*e*[1].

Fullers Chamber — Item an olde Fetherbedd wyth ij newe patchys a blankett An olde hanginge of Red saye wyth a border A Strayle.

Nutting*is* Chamber — Item a fetherbed a woolleyn blanket a grete whyte quylte wythe leaves and trees.

Busbyes Chamber — Item a fetherbed A large bolster A payer of good wolleyn blanketis. — Busby est r̃

Patchys Chamber — Item a fetherbed a bolster a pyllowe | An olde coverlet of grene Tapstre worke An olde carpet. — datur Sibilla Wylson vidua geven to the said wydowe beyinge a very pore woman

m[um] alle this Stuffe conteyned in this Inuentory the plate excepte, ys the Priors & of his owne prouysion

Thys is the Inuentory declareyng the plate the beddyng and other Stuff that belongyth vnto me Dan Dionise Dalyons Prior of the Monastery of Seynt Peter at Westm*inster*[2].

In primis at the entryng into my house iij f*our*mys and ij Lathers. — pro Dalione

Item in the Garden twoo Styllatoryes. — pro Decano

[1] 'John Portonari (see Suppr. of Monasteries, 180; comp. Dom. Pap. Henry VIII, III, p. 11, fo. 1535).' M. E. C. W.

[2] See the discussion (pp. 50 ff.) as to the site of the Prior's House. The portions taken over by the new dean, especially the furniture of the chapel, should be noted, as confirming the conclusion that when the dean was obliged to give up the Abbot's House to the new bishop he in his turn displaced the prior.

In the Kechyn.

Pro Dalione — In primis a barre (*remayneth*) of Iron | a payre of Rackis (pro Priore) and iij pothokis.

Item a trevett | a gyrdyron and a boylyng lead (remayneth).

Item ij Spytt*is* ij Dryppyng pans | and a brason ladle.

Item a pele of Iron*e* | a Skomer | and a cleveyng knyf.

Item vj brason pott*is* | a Chaffer and iij pannys.

Item a kettle and a frying pane.

In the Bottrye.

Pro Dalione — In primis ij pewter Saltt*is* and a pewter pottell pott.

Item a pynt pott of pewter | and v. Candelstyck*is* of latten*e*.

Item ix platters v. dysshes. v sawcers | iiij pottengers of pewter.

Item a byn*e* for brede (re*mayneth*) | ij Chest*is* (j re*mayneth*) and a Chaffyng dyshe.

Item v. Drynkyng glasses | iij kylderkyns | and a payle.

Item iij table clothes oon of them Dyap*er* and the other ij pleyn*e*.

Item vj Dyaper napkyns, viij napkyns of pleyn*e* clothe and iij pleyne towell*is*.

In the Hall. — xiij.s. iiijd.

sold to the Deane — In primis Hangingis of old grene say | ij olde banckers and a standyng Cupbard.

Item ij tables, j payr*e* of trestell*is* | ij fourmys and a hangyng Laumpe.

In the Parler. — vj.s. viijd.

sold to the Deane — In primis a complete hangyng of olde worn*e* saye with a border of antyke work to the same belongyng.

Item ij cupbordis with a carpett on euery on*e* of them. (j & ij carpett*is* dantur Dalion*e*)

Loste — Item an old Carpett in the Wyndoo.

Dantur Dalioni — Item a table ij trestyll*is* and a carpett longyng to y[e] same.

Item ij fourmys ij cheyres and ix Joynyd stoll*is*.

Dantur Dalioni — Item vij quysshons | ij awndyrons and a fyre pan*e*.

Item a fyre Forke and a peyre of bellowes.

In the Chappell.

geven — Item Fyrst iij Vestment*is* (recepit Decanus) withowte albys | a wrytten masse boke (n[t]) | a super altare (recepit Decanus) & a lytle Crucifixe (recepit Dalion).

Item a lytle Empty Chest and ij pec*is* of grene saye. (recepit Decanus.)

In the Fyrst Chambre.

Dantur Dalioni — In primis a complete hangyng of old worne saye and bokeram payntyd.

Item a testour of lynnyn clothe peyntyd.

sold to the Deane — Item a bedsted (*remayneth*) and a fourme (*remayneth*)— ijs. iiijd.

Item a cheyre of Joynyd Worke | a Desk and a Cupberd.

Item a peyre of Awndyrons and a mappe.

Item a Fetherbed a bolster and a Couerlett lynyd wyth Sowltwyche and a mantell apone the same bed.

In the second Chambre.

Dantur Dalioni — In primis a newe complete hangyng of sowltwyche staynyd.

Item a Sparner of Dornix very old.

Item a bedsted a mattresse | ij blankett*is* | ij peyre of straylli*s* ij lynyd couerlett*is* ij bolsters and a pyllowe.

Item vj Chest*is* grett and small | a Joynyd cheyre and a fourme.

Item a bason of Pewter.

Item ij stamell*is* ij Doblett*is* a Cloke | a longe gown and a hose clothe.

Item ij Cott*is* of clothe one of them furryd and a cote of Say wythowte slevys.

Dantur Dalioni — Item vij peyre of Shett*is* | iij shyrtt*is* and v pyllow beres.

Item vij kerches viij handkerches and iij course wypeyng towell*is*.

Item ij Cappes | ij brusshes | and ij curteyns of grene bokeram.

Plate.

[In primis a Flatt peace of syluer parcell gylte white.

Item xij spones, x of one sorte and ij of another sort.]

Item vj old masers wth bond*is* of syluer and gylt v. of them haveyng bossys.

[Item a couer of wood peyntyd seruyng for a maser haveyng at the end therof a kuppe of syluer and gylte.]

Datur Dalioni — Item a Salte of Syluer [parcell gylt] (white) without a couer.

vj Dantur Dalioni — Item xij Spones white and a flatte pece white ponderis— xxxix oz.

ij Dantur Dalioni — Item vj masores. — vj Spones ponderis—v. oz. di*midium* and one flatte pece ponderis—viij oz. and iiij masoures delyuered to M[r] Treasorer to the Kyngis vse.

In the masshyng house[1] — In primis ij furnesses of copper | A bygger and a lesser.

Item a masshe twnne.

Item ij Rudders.

[1] The brew-house.

Item a tappe hose and a tapstaf.
Item a grete collender | A meddlyng showyll.
Item a penyall batche[1] | A lyker batch.
Item v tynes to bere ale.
Item a wort collender and a houell.
Item a gyest[2] to set ale apon.
Item ij fyre pyckes and ij fyre hookis.
Item ij fyre rak*is* and ij fyre shovels.
Item a worte troughe *of lead*[3].

In thomelis chamber — Item ij old myll stones.

In Saynt Johns House — In primis iij peynted clothes | a table | and ij formes and ij benches.
Item iiij bynnes to put malt yn and ij malt baskett*is*.

In the mylhouse — In primis a myll with a trough.
Item a tubbe | ij treys and a sacke.
Item ij *old*[3] horses *wherof one ys blind*[3] with the harneys perteynyng to ye same.
Item ij whelebarouse.
Item an old mylstone.
Item a dong forke.

In the godd*is* blessing house — In primis ij tubbes and a samon barell.
Item lxxvij kymnels[4].
Item a gyest.

In the Ealing House — In primis iiij grete ealing tunnes set with ledde rond about.
Item an old tubbe | and a clensing stole | a tabret of lede.
Item v. scooppes | ij ale gyestis | iij metyngstandis one of x galons an other of vij and the other of iiij galons.
Item a tabret of wodde with a hoke of yron. Item ij tres with ij peyr of hookis to bere ale with.

In the bake House — In primis a pan of copper couered with bord*is* | an oven stocke of yron. Item a gret molding bord and a gret troughe.
Item iij bords to set bred on. Item ij old bults | x. sack*is* good and badde | A turne with a spyndle of yron.
Item a brake.
Item a pere of scales with a weight of led.
Item an old busshell.
Item a payle of iiij galons.
Item an old Ambery.
Item a pan which is at the kyng*es* past*er*ye with a trough.

[1] A vessel to brew penny ale in.
[2] 'A Juste to set Ayle one,' below, p. 46. Probably the same word as 'joist.'
[3] The italicised words are additions in another hand.
[4] A kimnel is a kind of tub.

Memorandum the [Deanes] (Abbottes) Chamber furnysshed complete geven vnto hym by the Kyngis Comissioners[1].

THE INVENTORYE OF THE GOODIS IN THE COVENT KYCH[EN].

In primis ij greate boyellers of brase standyng In the furnes.

Item v. brase Pottis Euery one of quantety bygger then other.

Item a litle brase pote.

Item a greate chaffer of bullen mettell[2] with ij handellis and withowte feete.

Item a lesser chaffer of the same mettell with ij Eyeres and iij feete.

Item iiij brase pannes Euery one bigger then other | itche of them banded with Irone and ij Eyres.

Item a litle old brase pane vnbownd.

Item a skeuer shafted withe wood.

Item ij cowrsers, a mynsyngknyff, ij leychyng knyffis, and a choppyng knyff.

Item a fleshe howke of Irone.

Item a collender.

Item a brazen morter, with a pestell of Irone.

Item a chaffyng dyshe.

Item a greate bred grayte.

Item a greate gredyrone with xj barres.

Item a fyere shovell, and a colrake of Irone shaftid with wood.

Item a peyre of Irone rackis.

Item a longe greate tryvet of Irone with vj feete and iiij Irone barres.

Item a greate pane for froyes of bullen mettell.

Item a greate fryeng pane with a slyce of Irone.

Item iiij greate spittis, iij skware and one rownd.

Item ij smale spittis for Eles.

Item an Irone peele shaftid with wood.

Item an axe, and iij Irone Wedges.

Item a old greate cubbard, standyng In the Kychen.

Item a new cowpe.

Item a greate morter of stone, with a pestell of wood.

Item ij greate tubbes to water fyshe In.

Item a cubbard at the frater hole[3].

Item a [greate] longe drepyng pane.

Item a litle Safferne bottell of tyne.

[1] This appears to mean that the Abbot's Chamber (shewn on the plan at p. 6) was treated as the private room of Dean Benson (Abbot Boston), and that no inventory of its contents was taken.

[2] So above, in the Abbot's kitchen, we had 'Bulleyn Mettell,' p. 35.

[3] 'The frater hole,' or hatch communicating with the kitchen, may still be seen in the south wall of the refectory.

In the salt Howse.

Item ij bynnes for bey salte.
Item ij barrellis for whytsalte.
Item a otemeyle tube with a peke of otemeyle.
Item a spayd.
Item a kylderkyn of varges.

In the blake parlor.

Item a standyng bord.
Item a old chest.
Item ij old skymeris.
Item iij stand*is* for Ayle.
Item a Juste to set Ayle one.

In the Wetlarder.

Item ij broyene-tubb*is*. Item a old cubbard. Item iij grete booll*is*.
Item a greate tube standyng, In the entry, to hang meate.
Item ij hand baskett*is*.

[Ornamentis of] Plate gifyn by kyng Henry the vij[th] to the Hovse of Westm*inster*.

Fyr*st* a gret Image of *our* Lady gylte—cccxxij oz. d.
Item one Chalys of gold ponderis—xxxvij oz.
Item iiij chalys gylt.
Item vj chall*is* p*ar*cell gylt.
Item vij pere of Cruett*is* gylt.
Item vj sacryng bell*is* gylt.

The Inuentory of the Stuffe perteynyng to the Offyce of the Farmari[1].

The parlare.

The hangyngis of Red and grene say ij Tabullis ij payer of Trestullis vj cusshyns of Tapartry with a torne banker ij fote Fourmys A peyer of Aundeyrons A payer of bellowys A cheyr A Joyned stole.

The Chamber over the Parlar.

The hangyngis of grene saye with a border Aboue. A bedsted with a blewe Sparner A blewe corteyne before the wyndowe A cupbord A litle old bord | ij old Chestys A turnyd Cheyer A fote pase A litle paynted clothe.

The Chamber ouer the botrye.

The Hengyng*is* of Red saye with a bordar aboue. A bedsted with a peynted sparuer A scholf A Joyned benche with Awnberes A fote fo*ur*me A lytle presse And yron grate in eche Wyndowe.

[1] *i.e.* the Infirmary in the Little Cloister.

The grete Parlar with saynt Kateryns Gardyn.

[The Hangyng*is* of] A Table an*e* old cupbord A close Benche.

The Chamber next the sayd Parlar.

The Hangyng*is* peynted Clothes A Bedsted ij shellff*is*.

The study w*ith*in the same gardyn.

The Hangyngis peynted clothes | A Rounde benche | iij shelff*is*.

The Sykmens Chamber*is*.

The Fyrste hangyd with peynted Clothes A Bedsted with a sparner | A table | ij Trestyll*is* | A tournyd cheyer | A forme ij benchys | ij shelffis. The Second Chamber hangyd with payntyd Clothes | A Bedsted with a blewe Sparner an old Chayer an old table with fete.

The Hall.

The Hangyng*is* of grene saye | ij old torne Bankers | A Broken cupbord ij Tables standing vppon trestellis one forme | A Round table for oysters. A turnyd Cheyer.

Seynt Kateryns Chappell
within the Farmarye.

F. Adames executor Testamenti Doctoris Gorton

[A pix of latyn with] a Canapye for the Sacrament | A litle
Datur Ecclesie
Box of syluer without a couer | A Chalesse with a pa(te)n And vj corporax casis. v. corporac*is*. A westment of Russut satten with a crosse of red Damask And borderyd with crymissyn*e*Welloett with And Albe And all thyng Belongyng | A Westement of Red Damask. The crosse Whyte Damask with Albe And All thyng belongyng iiij old Westment*is* with on*e* Albe and other thyngs for on*e* Westment.

m^um^ one Vestment geven to the Churche of Stanes

iij course Awter clothes with iij front*is* One Awter cloth with a front of Whyte and redd Damask with ane ymage of Seynt Erasmus and

iiij appoynted to the Churche

lynen
saynt Laurence[1] sett with perll*is* and stone, viij [lyned] Auter clothes with ij short hand Towell*is* | And old Carpett apon the auter A Crucifyx of wod. A table of the dome iij laten candelstyk*is* An holy water stock of laten with the sprynkyll of wod ij cruettis of peuter. On candelstyk of yron And iiij candelstycckis in the wall. j myssale with on*e* desk

[1] It is probable that the building, or at least the completion, of the Infirmary and St Katharine's Chapel in the twelfth century was due to Abbot Laurence (1158—73). He appropriated to the Infirmarer the churches of Battersea and Wandsworth; and his anniversary had in consequence to be provided by that officer. Moreover there was an altar of St Laurence in St Katharine's Chapel (Customary, p. 246).

ij Bokis ij Bokis for seynt Kateryne A Joyned stole with ane old lytell forme | ij deskis with ij old book*is* to saye *ser*uice Apon | a Sacring Bell with a ...tt Bell, A lampe hengyng with a Corde...paxe, ij Blow curtyns before the ymagys | ij curtyns for the Auter of whyte and red sarcynet | ij Gret chestis with an old payer of Organs without pypes. A bere with a cofyn for Ded men | ij Tabul*is* in the syde chappell*is* Apon the Auters | An old chest in the chappel.

The Chappel Chamber.

The Hangyng of payntyd clothes A Bedsted with a Sparner. A close cheyr with a old forme.

Stuffe Remaynyng in the botry.

First a syluer salt with a couer Item xij Syluer sponys on*e* maser ij Basons A standyng Nutte with a cover. ij Basons with one ever of pewter. Item a laten bason with An ewer A quart pott All for wyne. Item an Ale pott cont*eynyng* iij pyntis. Item a mattok with one spade. Item ij Tabull clothys ij towellis. Item vj Candelstyckis. Item vj napkyns.

Stuffe Remaynyng in y[e] kechyn.

Furst pannys and kettullis iiij. Item pott*is* of bras iiij. Item a chafur. Item a [geven to Dalyon] brasyn morter. Item vij platts. Item v. dysshes. Item iij sawcers Item a chafyng dysshe Item a brasyn ladyll. Item a laten scom*er*. Item a payer of Awndeyrons. Item a fyre sholue. Item a ...wderyng[1] tubbe ij tryvittis. Item a fryyng pan*e*. Item ij drepyng pannys.

Plate in the fermory.

Datur Decano — Item vj masours of sundry sort*is*.
Item a nutte with a couer gilte.

Item xij Spones [wherof one ys gilte] ponderis—xiiij oz. — Deliberantur Thesaurario ad vsum domini Regis
Item a salte with a cover parcell gilte. ponderis—vij oz. d.

cancellatur quia datur Dalion — [Item a large greate masour] garnys.

Lackynge [Lackynge Busshell] — Item a chalyce gilte.

Plate in the Hostery.

geven to the Deane — Item a salte with a couer gilte. ponderis—viij oz. — Deliberatur Thesaurario
Item vj syluer spones.

[1] Probably 'a powderying tubbe' (salting tub), as above, p. 36.

white ponderis—vij oz. Deliberatur Thesaurario
one
Item iij masoures wherof one ys a Stondyng masour. Deliberatur Thesaurario
Item a white pece of syluer ponderis—ix oz.

Item a Masour boll callid [the] Seynt Edwardis Masour garnysshed with siluer. Deliberatur Thesaurario

geven to the Deane iij Item vj white pecis of syluer pounced in the bottone. iij Deliberantur Thesaurario ad vsum Regis ponderis xlvi oz.

Westminster Plate reseruyd for the Kyngis Maiestie[1].

Churche plate Furste, a payre of greate syluer Sensoures, gilte po*nderis*— cclxxiiij oz.

Item the vth myter of white cloth garnysshed complete with floures of syluer gilte of dyuerse sortes with stones complete with Labell*is* of the same worke and garnysshed weyinge alle togethers— xvj oz.

Item the vj^{th} myter for seynt Nicholas Bysshoppe the grounde therof of white sylk garnysshed complete with Floures greate and smalle of syluer and stones complete in them with the scripture Ora pro nobis S*anc*te Nicholace embroded theron in p*er*le the sydes syluer and gilte and the Toppis of syluer and gilte and enamyled with ij Labellis of the same garnysshed in lyke maner and with viij large bellis of syluer gilte weyinge all togethers— xxv oz.

Item one Pecturalle of syluer gilte, garnysshed complete with course stones and perles wantynge twoo stones hauinge ane angell at the syde and three Pyctures in the Myddeste of syluer gilte ponderis-- xij oz.

Item a Bason of Agatha garnysshed with golde and xj greate stones with their collettis of golde and with v. other collett*is* of golde garnysshed with smalle stones and perles and iiij greate perles and vppon the bakesyde v. *faces* of golde alle weyinge togethers— xxxviij oz.

Item a Crowne of syluer gilte with iiij Crosses and iiij flowre de Luc*is* with Doble wrethes, aboute and betwene the wrethes flowres enamyled complete rounde aboute stondynge of viij Jemous alle weyinge to gethers xliiij oz. d.

Item iij endes of a broken crosse of beralle with boltes of yorne garnysshed with syluer and gilte weyinge alle to gethers lxx oz.

Item a payre of Candelstykkis gilte ponderis—

Item a Crucifix stondyng opon of syluer gilte.

[1] This Inventory belongs to the earlier set printed by Walcott, and repeats items therein contained. It is given here for the sake of completeness.

Item twoo basones of syluer gilte.

Howssholde plate

Item a bason and an*e* ewre of syluer parcell gilte po*nderis*—

Item a salte wit*h*oute a couer of syluer parcall gilte viij square prynted with Roses and Parcoleys, po*nderis*—

Item twoo Drynkynge sortable Cuppis withoute couers chequyred po*nderis*—

Item a lytell Drynkynge Cuppe of syluer white—

Item a stondynge nutte withoute a couer of sylluer gilte hauynge a man sleppynge a tree in the Toppe of the couer po*nderis*—

Item a greate stondynge Nutte with a foote garnysshed and a Couer of syluer gilte with an acorne in the Toppe po*nderis*—

H.

The Dean's House in the Bishop's time.

The monastery was surrendered 16 Jan. 1540, and on 17 Dec. the new charter founded a bishopric with dean and chapter. Wm Benson, the late abbot, was the new dean, but his house was granted to the bishop on 20 Jan. 1541. An inventory was taken of its furniture on behalf of the king: part was sold and part granted to the bishop or the dean. (See above, pp. 30—41.)

The bishop received, besides the mansion of Cheynygates, the buildings called the *Calbege* and the *Blackestole*, being from the Gateway Tower to the Blackestole Tower (not inclusive) 88 ft.: also all buildings between these on the west and 'le Frayter Misericorde' and the Kitchen on the east. Further, he had a stone tower and great barn in the Oxehall, and other buildings and gardens to the south-west. He also had the west cloister walk.

But the Frater, the Misericorde, the Kitchen, the Granary with its tower, the Brewhouse and the Bakehouse, were not given to the bishop. All these, and the rest of the precincts, were given to the dean and chapter.

It would be most natural to suppose that the dean would have the prior's house, which was considerable in extent, as the Inventory shews. But hitherto we have been unable to fix the position of this house: for Walcott's suggestion that it was 'on the north-east side of the Little Cloister' cannot be entertained. We must therefore follow other clues.

The first mention of the Dean's House occurs in Chapter Book I, f. 15 *a*: *water is to be brought to* my Lord's kitchen, *Mr Dean's kitchen,* and various houses of prebendaries and others, as well as to the church and 'saxtri' (26 Jan. 1544).

The next order to be noted comes nearly two years later, 15 Dec. 1545; and the dean must by that time have settled into his house, wherever it may have been. This order (f. 28 *a*) in fact gives us the first clue to its position. 'That Mr Dean and his successors shall have *the Misericorde, the Great Kitchen,* and *all edifices betwixt his own House and the School,* and *the Great Garden* with the pond and trees, which he hath now in possession.'

The same day it was ordered that 'Mr Haynes shall have pertaining to his house, to him and his successors, all the garden enclosed in the stone wall, with the old dovehouse, and the house called Canterbury, with the garden ground from his house to *Mr Dean's garden.*'

Three years passed, and then we read, 15 Dec. 1548 (f. 48 *b*), 'that it shall be lawfull for Mr Dean to take down the timber and tiles of two broken chambers standing beside the Schoolhouse: and also that he shall have *the ground of the Frater*[1] with the stone walls to the augmentation of his garden: and also *that his garden in the Farmery,* and also *the Chambers joining to his house of the Dorter side unto the Abbot's Lodging*[2]. And that Mr Haynes shall have immediately the house with the garden and dovehouse, heretofore granted him.'

These notices make it clear that Dean Benson on leaving the abbot's house betook himself to a house which was on the south side

[1] The order to pull down the Frater 'forthwith in all hast for the avoiding of further inconveniens' had been made on 5 November 1544.

[2] This expression, 'unto the Abbot's Lodging,' occurring in this context has much exercised me. For some time I thought it must mean 'as an addition to the Dean's house,' the word 'Abbot' having come in by a slip for 'Dean,' as William Benson who had been abbot did not die till the next year. But such a mistake appeared improbable after a period of eight years. I now believe that the solution is to be found by bringing side by side with it another puzzling expression, 'the camera of the lord abbot in the dormitory,' which I have recently found in a roll of Henry VIIth's time. *Munim.* 24, 281 is an account roll of John Islip, receiver of the abbot [viz. John Esteney], of the year 1496. On a slip attached we read: 'Memorandum quod rem', in una cista in camera domini abbatis in dormitorio, in pecuniis numeratis de pecuniis predict' domini abbatis et sub custodia fratris Johannis Yslyp, xxiii° die Octob' anno xii° Regis Henrici vii¹, DCᵗI.' It would thus appear that the abbot retained a chamber in or adjoining the dormitory, perhaps with a view to an occasional conformity with the ancient rule by which he was required to sleep with his monks; possibly also for his own convenience when he had let the Abbot's Place to the widowed queen. The term 'unto the Abbot's Lodging' will thus mean, 'as far as the old camera of the abbot in the dorter.'

of the refectory, and that various accessories were added to his portion by chapter orders. These accessories were

1. The Misericorde, the site of which we must discuss presently.
2. The Convent Kitchen.
3. Buildings between his house and the School (*i.e.* the present house of the headmaster).
4. The College Garden, which had been the Infirmary Garden.
5. The site of the Refectory.
6. Certain chambers next to his house and to the Dormitory.

The site of Ashburnham House exactly suits the position to which most of these accessories point, and there is no other that will. If confirmation of this site be needed, it will be found presently in the lease which was made of the 'Dean's House,' when the dean got possession of the abbot's house at the reconstitution under Queen Elizabeth.

It is evident that the new dean secured for himself the lion's share of the divisible territory after the bishop's requirements had been met. The new chapter contained six of the old monks and six clerics from outside. Five of the latter obtained the first five stalls; then came Dionysius Dalyons, the former prior, in the sixth stall, followed by the five other monks: another outsider had the twelfth stall. The chapter orders of the earliest period contain interesting notices which enable us to discover a good many of the houses in which these new prebendaries were settled. Obviously the prior, who came sixth on the list, could not expect to keep his old house, which the Inventory shews us to have been of considerable extent. It is, as we have said above, natural to suggest that the prior's house went to the new dean; and the suggestion is placed beyond reasonable doubt when we observe in the Inventory how large a portion of its furniture is noted as having been sold or given to the Dean.

We now give an extract from the first lease of the 'Dean's House' (Reg. v. f. 70), which offers interesting topographical details.

This Indenture the xxvi[th] daie of March in fourth yere of the raigne of our soveraigne Ladie Elizabeth...betwene Gabriell Goodman Deane of the Church Collegiate of saint Peter in Westm[r] and the Chapitor of the same place of thone partie, and Dame Anne Parrie wydowe, late wief of Sir Thomas Parrie knighte, disceassed, and William Norrys of Jolly John in the countie of Berks Esquyer, and Thomas Bromeley of the Inner Temple in London gent of the other partie Wytnesseth that the said Deane and Chapitor...for and in consideracion of the surrendre...of one greate mansion house or messuage sett lying and beinge within the precincte and close of the late dissolved Monasterie of Westm[r]...late in the teanure and occupacion of the said Sir Thomas Parrye knighte...and of all houses, barnes, stables, orchards, gardens, edificons, and buyldinges belonging or in any wise appertayninge to same greate mansion house or messuage, have demised...unto the said Dame Anne Parrye all that their house or messuage comenly called or knowen by the name of the Deanes house, sett, lying and beinge within the said precincte...now in the teanure or occupacion of the said Deane with all houses, Chambres, lodgings, edifices and buildinges to the said mansion house or messuage onlye in any wise belonging or apperteyninge, And also one greate Chambre called the misericord, and all that their kytchynne comenly called or knowen by the name of Covente kytchynne with a lytle severall courte to the same kytchynne adioyninge and lyinge on the south syde of the same kytchyn and butting upon the schole house towerdes the weaste with all other houses offices edifices comodities and buildinges to the said greate covente kytchyn in any wise belonginge or apperteyninge, And also one pryvie adioyning to the said scole house and to the said lytle Courte, And also all that their gardyne lyinge betwene the said house called the Deanes house and the greate cloister on the south and north partes, And also the free use profyte and comoditie of the water conduite within the saide house called the Deanes house, And also two stables and one barne now in the occupacion of the said dame Anne, And also free waie with passage from the saide house called the Deanes house unto the Church called Westm[r] Church, and free waie and passage from the same Church unto the said house called the Deanes house....Except...one Chambre scituate and being at the easte ende of the galerie within the said Deanes house leading by a stayre into the covente garden there, And also one other rowme or chambre there adioyninge to the said Chambre on theast side therof, And also all houses, all granaries, stables, buildinges and edifices scituate and beinge on the weaste syde of the waie leading from the saide Deanes house unto the gate there leading into the bowlyng Alley.... To have, hold...during the naturall lyef of the said Dame Anne Parrye, and...unto the said Thomas Bromeley and William Norrys...from the day of the death of the said Dame Anne Parry unto thend and tearme of sixe yeres...yealdinge...three poundes sixe shillinges and eighte pence....

The Dean's House was afterwards in the occupation of William Norrys; then of Sir John Fortescue; and in 1621 of his granddaughter Jane Poulteney. Then the remainder of the lease was assigned to Sir Edw. Powell for £1000 in 1628, and he had a new lease in 1629. In this lease (*Munim.* 35,772) we find the following additional clauses:

One peece of ground lying on the west side of the said...Deanes house, contayning in length on the west side towards the Schoolemaisters Garden Thirtie seven foote, and in breadth from the said house att the South end towards the way leading from the said house to the Colledge yeard fowerteene foote, and in breadth from the South west Corner of the ould Kitchen westwards Eight foote of assize, which said peece of ground is latelie built uppon.

Except...two Chambers scituate lying and being att the East end of the Gallary within the said house...sometymes leading by a staire into the Covent Garden there; both which are now converted into a great paire of staires and a passage into the new Schoole house there.

* * * * * * * * * * * * * *

As well all that theire Roome with thappurtenances as it is now severed and devided...being under part of the Schoole house...and the same abutteth upon the way or passage that leadeth from the great Cloysters unto the little Cloysters...on the West and South parts, and upon the lodgings of Doctor Robinson and late of Mr Hacklute on the East part, and upon a Colehouse or place for wood late in the tenure...of William Neile gent deceassed on the North part, and the said demised Roome is...now or late used for a Colehouse or place to laye wood in: (also a woodhouse under the Gate leading from the said demised house into the Colledge Yeard and being over the Comon Sewer there).

The later story of this house is told by Mr Harry Sirr in his valuable paper on *Ashburnham House* in *Journal of R.I.B.A.*, vol. xvii, no. 5, where a conjectural plan of its condition in Elizabethan times is given.

I.

The Site of the Misericorde.

When Walcott published the Suppression Inventories, he drew a tentative plan of the monastic buildings by the aid of scattered notices found in these Inventories, in the first Chapter Book and in the mutilated MS of Abbot Ware's Customary. Ever since that time the Misericorde has been identified with a long range of buildings running parallel with the Refectory and separated from it by about 50 feet of open ground. Practically the whole of this range is now included in the southern portion of Ashburnham House.

When Mr Micklethwaite wrote his *Notes on the Abbey Buildings at Westminster*, he accepted this identification of the site of the Misericorde. He regarded the point as settled by the terms of the grant made to Bishop Thirlby of the abbot's house in 1541. Apart from this he would have been inclined to place the Misericorde at the west end of the Refectory, in a position similar to that of the 'Loft' at Durham which served the same purpose.

The question deserves a more accurate treatment than it has hitherto received; and the publication of the Customary facilitates the enquiry. This important document belongs to the period before the great fire of 1298, which seriously injured the monastic buildings, and led to their ultimate reconstruction, which was only completed under Abbot Litlyngton a century later.

In the Customary we find the terms *domus misericordiae* (pp. 83,

101, 123 bis, 131 bis, 134 ff., 177), and *misericordia* in the same sense (pp. 100, 124, 130 f., 178). Moreover the following sentences occur:

p. 149. The cellarer must maintain in repair not only the roof of the dorter, &c., but also 'tecturam, mensas et fenestras refectorii atque illius domus eidem contiguae, quae misericordia vocatur.'

p. 227. Abbot Richard Ware in 1275 ordered 'ne unquam de cetero fratres laici conversi cum fratribus in domo quae misericordia nuncupatur aliquo modo publice aut privatim loquantur.'

p. 229. A mutilated sentence regarding the 'fratres conversi' ends with the words, 'in refectorio maxime, aut in domo quae juxta refectorium misericordia nuncupatur.'

A passage on p. 135 mentions the lights required in the Misericorde, and also the serving-hatch towards the kitchen:

Et, quia de misericordiae domo superius fit mencio, sciendum quod inter cenandum tempore misericordiae tres super mensam cerei accendentur, et super quemlibet cereum duae candelae ponentur accensae, et duae ad fenestram hinc inde accendentur, una videlicet interius et altera ex parte coquinae: quas quidem octo candelas singulis noctibus subsacrista portabit ibidem.

A certain sacrist is severely blamed (p. 136), who had once, 'indecenter,' caused lights to be carried into the Misericorde from tables in the Refectory at which but few brothers were dining.

The Customary of St Augustine's Canterbury, which is derived from that of Westminster, seems to indicate that the Misericorde there was in the Infirmary. It is called 'domus misericordiarum' in the *Reformaciuncula* of Abbot Nicholas de Spina (1273—1283), which forms one of the earlier portions of the book; and in the later part, where the Westminster book is followed, the Misericorde is omitted from the list of buildings (p. 195) which the cellarer has to maintain.

We gather then that in the 13th century the Misericorde at Westminster was a building contiguous to the Refectory, and had a serving-hatch by which food was served from the kitchen. It seems therefore that the site suggested by Mr Walcott, and generally accepted, cannot be justified for the earlier period before the time of Abbot Litlyngton.

In his description of the probable site of the kitchen (*Notes*, p. 30), Mr Micklethwaite notices 'a Norman wall running from the south side of the Frater [at right angles to it, and a little east of the existing serving-hatch], in which wall are two round-headed windows, high up, which shew it to have been the east side of a building.' This building, he thinks, was not the kitchen, but may have been the larder. Is it not possible that this, or at least the upper part of it, was the Misericorde?

The next document with which we have to deal is nearly three centuries later, and we must allow for the possibility of the rebuilding of the Misericorde, and even for the possibility of a new site. By letters patent of King Henry VIII, 20 Jan. 1541, the newly constituted bishop of Westminster was granted the abbot's house, called Cheynygates, and certain other parts of the monastic buildings[1]. Among these were 'the Calbege' and 'the Blacke Stole,' which together formed the northern portion of the long range on the east side of the present Dean's Yard, extending to 'the Blacke Stole Towre,' 88 ft. from the entrance tower under which is the passage to the cloister:

Ac omnia edificia terras et solum existentia inter predicta edificia vocata le Calbege et le Blackestole ex parte occidentali et edificia et domos vocatas le ffrayter misericorde et magnam coquinam conventualem vocatam le greate covent kechen dicti nuper monasterii ex parte orientali.

This portion seems to have been a yard with certain minor buildings to which no particular name could be attached, lying between the Calbege and Blacke Stole on the west and the Misericorde and kitchen on the east. The order in which the boundary buildings are mentioned suggests that the Misericorde was north of the kitchen, just as the Calbege was north of the Blacke Stole. There is certainly nothing in this description which fixes the Misericorde in the position generally assigned to it. The site above suggested, next to the Refectory, would, however, suit the words admirably well.

The 'Mysericorde' is mentioned in one of the Suppression Inventories printed above, but no indication is given as to its site.

We pass now to the earliest Chapter Book, from which we have already quoted certain orders (above p. 51).

The order of 15 Dec. 1545, which assigns the Misericorde to the dean, appears to have been hitherto interpreted as if it were of a much earlier date and referred to the original provision of a residence for the dean. But plainly he is already in 'his own house,' and is also in possession of 'the great garden,' *i.e.* the present College Garden. Three additional portions are here assigned to him and his successors: the Misericorde, the Convent Kitchen, and the buildings between his own house and the School (*i.e.* the present house of the headmaster). It is most reasonable to suppose that the order in which these portions are enumerated is from north to south: so that once more we are led to place the Misericorde immediately south of the Refectory.

[1] See above, Appendix F.

On 26 Mar. 1562, after the dean had moved to the old Abbot's Place, there was granted a lease (from which we have quoted extracts above) to Lady Anne Parry, widow of Sir Thomas Parry, who surrenders 'one great mansion house within the precinct' [Vaughan's House], and gets 'the Deanes house...now in the teanure or occupacion of the said Deane...and also one greate Chambre called the misericord,' and the 'Covente kytchynne with a lytle severall courte...on the south syde of the same kytchyn and butting upon the schole house' (Reg. v, f. 70: cp. Ch. Bk. I f. 108 *b*).

On 2 Mar. 1571 we have an order (f. 141 *b*) 'that the howse whyche the Lady Anne Parye widow now hath in lease, which in tyme past was the deanes howse, shall after the expiracion of her lease be grauntid and assigned unto two of the prebendaries[1].' Immediately following this is the order:

Item it is decreed, that the olde kitchyn hertofore called the covent kytchin and a howse called in tymes past the Misericorde, now dimised among other thinges to the Ladye Anne parrye widow; and also the old chapell somtyme called St Katheryns chapell in the lesse cloistre shalbe taken down, and the tymbre and stuff thereof to be reserved to thuse of the College by thadvise of the surveiour of the same Colledge.

As Lady Anne Parry was responsible for repairs, a release had to be given her: and so we read (f. 142 *b*) under date 24 Mar. 1571:

A release to dame Anne parry etc. for the reparing of the great convent kitchyn and the Misericorde.

Two documents in the Register (VI f. 18) describe the surrender by Lady Anne Parry, Thomas Bromeley Esq., Solicitor General, and William Norres Esq., of the Misericorde and Kitchen, and their release from their obligation to repair them. Both bear the date 1 June 1571, though by error the xiith is written for the xiiith year of Queen Elizabeth. The terms in which the buildings are described are of importance; for they shew that the Misericorde was not on the ground-floor, but had beneath it certain premises belonging to the Kitchen.

(1) 'All that greate Chamber called the myssericorde, and all that kitchin comenlie called or knowen by the Name of the Covent Kitchin, and a lytle Severall Courte to the same kitchin adioyninge and beinge on the South syde of the same kitchin and abuttinge upon the Scole house towardes the Weste, and all other nouses, offices, edifices, Commodites and buyldinges beinge parcell of the same Covent Kitchinge in any wise belonginge or apperteyninge or beinge directelie under the saide Grete Chamber the misericordes.'

[1] This, as we have seen, was not carried into effect.

(2) Release from the repair of 'the greate Covente Kytchin and the Chamber callid the misericorde, and of all houses, edyfyces, bwyldinges dyrectlie under the said misericorde Chamber, and to the said Covente Kytchin belonginge or apperteyninge.'

This last item of information resolves what would have been a difficulty in our suggested identification of the site of the Misericorde: for almost immediately to the west of the Norman wall which we suppose to have been the east side of the Misericorde there still exists in the wall of the Frater a serving-hatch, supposed to be of the fourteenth century, and there appear to be traces, on the side of this hatch next to the kitchen, of the lower part of two vaulting shafts. If there was a vaulted chamber under the Misericorde which formed part of a passage to the kitchen, all the facts fit in well together.

If this suggestion should prove to be beset with difficulties of which I am not at present aware, I would fall back on the alternative possibility that the Misericorde was, as at Durham, a Loft at the west end of the Refectory. In any case, the two facts which are of decisive importance in the enquiry are that the Misericorde was 'contiguous' to the Refectory and that it was upstairs.

J.

Notices relating to the Deanery.

1. Chapter Book I f. 019 *v.*

'xxiv December 1565, a° Eliz. viii°. It is decreed by the dean and chapter that of xlviti. xiiis. ivd. remaining in thands of the said dean, of suche money as was graunted to the college by Gabriell Paulyn[1], there shall be bestowed as followeth by the discretion of M^r^ dean and Mr Yong, viz. All the hanging given by Mr Doctor Bill to the college shalbe lyned; the gallery chamber in M^r^ deanes lodging and the pallet chamber adioyning to the same shalbe furnished wt bed, bedding and other implements convenient to serve for the Electors of schollers and other like affaires of the college; and if the same money shall extende therunto, two silver potts of like fashion and weight as other of the college potts of silver be, shalbe bowghte to the college use.'

2. *Munim.* 39,389.

'Chardges &c.' of Thomas Fowler surveyor, Mar. 1575—6.

[1] See Register, p. 58, Covenant with G. Paulyne of Sheperton. May we identify him with Gabriell Palley, who is mentioned at the beginning of the Inventory (above, p. 30)?

Under 'Glassier': 'In the Audite house and under M[r] Deanes parler wyndow and in other places made of new glasse....'

Under 'Joyner': 'for making of Shelves for M[r] Deanes Chamber and Bracketes to them.'

3. *Munim.* 39,392. Similar 'Chardges,' Aug.—Oct. 1576.

'Plasterers occupied not only in Sellinge and Plastering the Seller and Thentry before the Kitchen, But also in whightwasshinge the Long gallerye....Matlaiers occupied in new mattinge of the Long gallerye and mending the Chamber where my Lord Russell did lye[1].'

'To Lewis Lizard for the new paintinge the Large gallery with blacke and whighte and the windows also being so letten by gret—xxxs.'

(Smyth) 'for mending a Candelsticke with a Joint for M[r] Deanes Chamber...for a double Casement for one of the Logings in the Corte under the parler.'

4. *Munim.* 40,192.

'for a hook to kepe open a gate in M[r] Deanes Coort—vid.'

5. *Munim.* Book 7.

A memoriall of sundrie things performed in five yeares by the Deane and Chapter of Westminster in the time of...Richard Neile....

....

1606. 1° Builded for the bettering of the Deane's lodginge: one Bedchamber and a Chimney in it, a pallett Chamber and a house of Office to yt with a bricke vault, the said Bedchamber wainscotted over and about the Chimney and the windowes and a wainscott Portall to yt.

[1] *John Lord Russell*: s. of Francis earl of Bedford who d. 1585. He m. in 1574 Elizabeth widow of Sir Thos. Hoby and d. of Sir Anthony Cook and sister-in-law to Cecil.

Elizabeth Lady Hoby must have been a friend of Dean Goodman: for in SPD Eliz. *Addenda* (1566—79) p. 6 there is a letter from Sir Th. Hoby to Sir W. Cecil (7 Apr. 1566) referring to the decayed state of Dover Castle: 'The Dn of Wm[r] who has conducted us so far, and has also been a witness of it, can testify thereto.' Eliz. Lady Hoby was with him, crossing the Channel. She mentions her 'cousin Wotton' as meeting them (he and Lord Montagu were returning from Bruges?). Hoby d. at Paris 13 July 1566.

She m. Lord Russell in 1574, and on account of the plague 'was allowed by the Dean to await her delivery in a house within the Precincts' (Stanley, *Memorials*, ed. 3, p. 219). 'Lord Russell's letter to the Queen announcing the birth is dated at Westminster College' (*ibid.*).

Ch. Bk. 9 Feb. 1582/3, Lease renewed to my Lord Russell.

He died 1584, and the learned Elizabeth his lady composed his epitaph in the Abbey.

2° Deane Goodman's ould Bedchamber seeled with deale, wainscott-wise and a large Presse in it and 3 new iron double rabited Casements putt into the windowe of that Chamber.

3° Twoe large Presses to laie apparall and necessaries in neere to the Deane's Chamber.

4° Part of the middle Chamber, betwixt the Bedchamber and the Studie wainscotted sutable to the Portalls there.

5° A studie with a Closett in it well furnished and fynished with shelves deske Table and the stone wall betwixt them and the shelves lined thorough with slitt deale, and a double Closett under the aforesaid new built Bedchamber made with shelves, a Presse and a great nest of great boxes for writings and papers, the Parlor somewhat enlarged, and 18 yardes of wainscott there sett upp sutable to the rest; The Cellers under Jerusalem with some other roomes elsewhere seeled with lime and haire.

6° The locks altered and some new plate lockes made and new kaies made thoroughout all the Deanes Lodgings:

Upon all which spent neere .200^{li}. for which the Colledge paid not past 100^{li}.

Item built for the Deanes use a large Stable sufficient to receave 16 Geldings with a haie loft over yt, a Coachehouse, a Saddlehouse and a Chamber for the Groomes and Coach-man, and a Gate-house neere to the Stable with a Chamber over yt, which is added to the Lawndresse's house all which cost about 100^{li}.

Item made in the Deane's little Gallerie .2. new large stoole windowes, the upper windowes in the Scholler's Chamber fitted with frames of wood and the same glased; A newe [Ji]nne (?) made for the Storehouse, and some tymber provided for necessarie uses about the Churche; All which coste the Some of 20^{li}.

....

Paid to the Bishopp of Elie that now is, and to Henrie Isackson his man for the wainscotting on the little Chamber on the foreside[1] of Jerusalem Chamber, and the making upp and glasing of the new stone windowe in that Chamber with the Armes in that windowe, and for the wainscotting that[2] Chamber and studie, in which Henrie Isackson lay with some other stuffe in that Chamber, as the Bill of the particulars will shewe—60^{li}.

Bestowed in anno 1606, in divers particulars, as the lyning of all the Colledge hanging thorough[3] with new strong canvas.

[1] A rough draft has 'farside.' [2] Draft: 'wenscot in the.' [3] Draft: 'through out.

2° divers Chambers and the Galleries newe matted.

3° the Bed in the Chamber on Jerusalem side furnished with a Rugg blanketts pillowes sheetes and pillowbeeres, Curtaines of greene kersey[1] lined with taffeta, and laced[2] sutable to the ould vallence of that Bedd.

4° Curtaines of draught worke and lined with buckeram to the windowes of that Chamber, and the like Curtaines for the great window of Jerusalem Chamber with Curtaine rodds hooks and rings to them in both Chambers.

5° and some twentie yardes of wainscott sett upp in Jerusalem Chamber, sutable to the rest of the wainscott there; to the some of 30^{li}.

....

Item in lewe of a Chest of Violls of 7^{li}. price, which I bought to have remained in the Colledge, I have and doe leave in the Deanes lodginge to become as Colledge goods, twoe great Standards bound with yron and twoe Locks upon each of them, the one standing in the Deane's new Beddchamber to locke upp the Colledge plate[3], the other in the Closett within the Deanes Studie for necessarie uses, Both being well worth 10^{li}.

6. Treasurer's Accounts for 1606.

'Item paied to Roger Edwards[4] for thinges provyded for the gallerye Chamber.	iiij^s vi^d
....	
Item paied for a Curtin of dorm[·] for the inner gallery Chamber with ii^s vj^d for Rings rope and makinge.	xvij^s viii^d
Item for three blanckets for the gallery at xvj^s a peece with vi^d for caryadge.	xlviij^s vj^d
....	
Item paied to Richd Ellison for matts for the gallerye and newe Chamber as appeareth by bill.	lxxiij^s ij^d
....	
Item paied to the late Deane for the wainescott in the Chamber over the Parlor and Studdye ther for two portalls and for wainescott in the Chamber at the ende of the gallerye by the garden and for a portall ther and for divers other parcells as by a bill therof made particularly appearethe[5].	xxii^{li} vij^s vj^d

(Side note by Neile, as follows:)

[1] Draft: 'Carsey.' [2] Draft: 'looped.' [3] Draft adds 'in.'

[4] He appears earlier as *vergifer*.

[5] This bill exists: see 'Reparations, 1606' (also the next two).

Mdn that neyther the mapes with liuerye bedsted on Jerusalem side, nor any part of any thinge left at Cheswicke, were any part of these things heer pd for, for the Deane pd for those twelve pounds besides.

Item paied to Henrye Isackson[1] for wainescott in the Chambers, Comonlye Called the Clerke of the Kitchins Chambers vizt the Inner Chamber and the Utter Chamber and for wainescott in the Studdye and for dores, Crosse garues, handles, locks, Casements, hings, bolts, srrnes (?), glasse, keyes, and dyvers other implements as by a bill therof made particulerly appearethe. } xxiv^{li}

(Side note by Neile, as follows:)

The Deane and Chapter thought good to pay for these things rather then to put the Coll servants to pay for them though the roomes be allotted for the registers and the Clerk of the Kitchin's lodginge.

....

(William Man, supervisor of works)...et pro expensis edificandi novum Cubiculum super Ambulacrum sive porticum iuxta aulam Collegii....'

7. Treasurer's Accounts for 1607.

'Item paied to John Clarke Joyner for 2 yards 2 foote of wainscott for the Chimney in Mr Deanes Studdy and for other things as appeareth by bill. } xxviij^{s}

....

For furnishing of the Colledge Bedd in Jerusalem syde' (full particulars follow).

8. Treasurer's Accounts for 1608.

'Item paid to Richd Ellison Upholster for divers necessaryes about Jerusalem side as appeareth by the bill of the particulers delivered me by Robt Knowles.' } vi^{li} x^{s} x^{d}

[1] He appears earlier as *clericus coquinae*, and also *procurator hospitii*: in 1607 Robert Knowles has taken his place.

9. Glazier's Bills for 1605/6 and 1606 give the following names of Chambers:

M[r] Deanes studye next the lyttell garden.
M[r] Deanes bed Chamber.
For the Nursery.
For the Closett next the Churche.
For the two newe wyndowes in the gallery.
(second bill) For M[r] Deanes greate chamber.
For the parlor.
For M[r] Deanes newe lodginges.

10. With the 'Memoriall' (no. 5) two other documents should be closely compared:

(1) *Munim.* 6611 (+ 6622), Inventory of Neile's time [*not* Goodman's].

(2) *Munim.* 6612, Inventory (embodying the former)—Mountain to Tounson, with notes of Williams's time, including payment for chimney-piece in Jerusalem.

(1)	(2)
New bedchamber	14
Pallet Chamber	15
M[r] Deane Goodmans olde bedchamber	16
Entry to the aforesaid newe bedchamber	13
Oratorie within M[r] Deane Goodmans bedchamber	17
Lobby betwixt the bedchamber and the middle Chamber	12
Middle Chamber	18
Studdy	19
Clossett within the Studdy	20
Clossett upon the midle of the Staires going to the aforesaid Chambers	11
Clossetts on the Gallerie Side—uttermost Clossett / Inner Clossett	10
Chamber betweene the Gallery and the Parlour	8
Gallerie Chamber	3
Little Chamber + Gallery	4+5
The great Chamber called Jerusalem	2
The Stone Gallery in the garden	6
The Parlour	7
Gallery neere the Parlour	9
Chamber over the Gate	23
Chamber called the nursery	21
Rogers Chamber	22
Hall	1

The figures on the right give the order of the rooms in (2), which contains also at the end: 'In the Chapter Clerkes and in the Clerke of the Kitchens Chamber and Studdie,' and 'In Henry Northedges Chamber.'

11[1]. *Munim.* 12,650 and 12,651.

Inventory of 'goods belonging to D[r] Williams yet remaining at Wm̃.' [1653].

2 dozen and halfe of Turky work Chaires.

2 dozen of woodden chaires with Penrhyn and Chockwillan armes thereon[2].

Severall peeces of gilt leather hangings now about the litle Gallery.

1 dozen of chaires suteable.

1 green suite of Curteyns Vallance and counterpanes.

6 peeces of Turky hangings.

Goods of his with M[r] Salloway.

....

12. *Munim.* 12,652.

In obedience to your Hon[rs] order of Satterday the 4th of June 1653.

I have perused the paper which I received from M[r] Williams his servant, and I finde that the 2 dozen and halfe of Turkey worke chayres there mentioned were belonging to the late Deane of Westminster D[r] Williams.

I finde the 2 dozen of wooden chayres with his armes painted on them which stood in the lower Gallery, to bee his.

The dozen of guilded leather chayres which stoode in the painted Gallery next to the Committy chamber to bee allso his.

The guilded leather Carpett which M[r] Salloway borrowed lying on a table in the same Gallery was his.

But for the guilded leather which hangeth about the other Gallery it hath beene there about the space of 30 yeares and I know not to whom it belongs.

And for any thing mentioned in the said paper besides these particulars they are none of my Lords.

This is certified to your honours grave wisdome by mee your hon[rs] humble servant,

Adam Brown.

[1] I have put this and the next two items in advance of their order, as they relate to Dean Williams.

[2] Second copy has: '2 dozen of woodden chayres in the low Gallery.'

13. *Munim.* 12,645.

Att the Comittee for the Colledge of Westm^{r} sittinge in the Deanes House in the said Colledge the 17th Day of Aprill 1646.

Whereas a Study of Bookes in the late Deanes House......ordered that Sir John Trevor (who hath the key of the said Study) be Desired forthwith to Deliver the Possession of the said Study of Bookes to the said Doctor Williams or to whom he shall appoint he first giveinge Security That after his Death they shall be sent to St John's Colledge in Cambridge accordinge to the former guift of the said Docter Williams.

14. *Munim.* 42,764 F.

18 October 1650, received of Mr Browne for making a doore way in the towar chambar[1], and mending the step, and finding the plaistar, the sum of 4s.

15. *Munim.* 42,765.

Aprill 27th 1650. A generall Bill for altering the Towar Chamber for the Right Honble the Lord President:

(1) The Carpenter. 'oen dower and tow gutters and puting tyes in the flower and Rafters in the Rowef...for takin up the flower and laying it....'

[1] This is the room in the S.W. Tower now called 'Bradshaw's Chamber'—recently dismantled. In Neile's *Memoriall* (see above, no. 5) we find: 'Bestowed an^{o} 1608, in the ould Belfrie over the Consistorie, in stone worke Iron worke bricke worke and timber worke to make an Evidence house, which is yet left unfinished, bestowed there—37li. 13s. 5d.' It would seem that some documents had been put into it, but that Dean Williams finding it was practically deserted made it into a chamber for his servant. For in the 'Heades for the Deanes Answer to the Objections of the 4 Junior Prebendaryes' we read: '*Ob.* 10. Item whereas it is enacted that the Registers and evidences which concerne the Churche be orderlye layd up in their distincte and severall places within some Roome appointed for that purpose as hath been formerlye accustomed, the said Lord Bishopp to make roome for his howsehold servante hath cawsed the said writinges and evidences to be remooved out of the place wherein they had before bin kepte, some to the private Custody of the Receivour Generall of the said Churche, and others to the dwellinge howse of the Chapter Clerke in the Towne of Westm^{r}, soe that wee knowe not whither to repaire upon anye searche, nor in what safetie the said evidences and writinges are. *Resp.* These lesser Evidences were alwayes kepte in the Custodye of our Register and Receivour Generall. And soe they are still. Our Charters and Endowments are safely kepte in our Muniment howse. Noe man but knoweth where to make his searche, and that more readilye then heretofore.' [*Munim.* 25,095.]

A Carpenter's bill in 1740 begins: 'In Laying on the Bridgings to the floor of Bradshaws Roome, Strikeing away the Scaffold to the North West Tower, Hoysting up the Stuff to the South West Tower, bording the window in Spirituall Court....'

(2) The Plumber. 'Two gutters of lead...new lead added unto ould.'

(3) The Bricklayer. 'taiking the Chimbley downe in the Towar and maiking the way to sett up a new one, finding nothing but workmanship, £1. 4. 6.'

[Total, £6. 3. 3.]

16. *Munim.* 42,766.

General bill for work done 'on the top of the two towers'[1]: £140. 'On the tower for building the roomes there': thirteen loads of oak (£25), new sheet lead (£48), fourteen casements (£7), 143 ft. of new glass (£4. 3. 0).

17. *Munim.* 42,766 (2).

'For setting upp a Rale at the topp of the Tower round about the stares.'

18. *Munim....*

Abstract of the severall Orders made touching the Deans House Westm^{r}.

Att a Meeting of the Governors of the Schoole and Almes Houses of Westm^{r}.

23 March 1649. Ordered vizt.

That the Roomes hereafter mencioned vizt, The Jerusalem Chamber the Lower and the upper Gallaries the two Chambers adioyning with the Garretts over them being all on the West Side of the late Deanes Howse with a Passage from the Hall to the Jerusalem Chamber and the Gardine adioyning be reserved for the use of the Governors for the tyme being and not to be Lett to any Person or Persons whatsoever.

Eodem Die.

That the Roomes hereafter mencioned vizt, The Hall 'the Buttery and Pantry the Cellars the Kitchin the Pastorie and the Larder with convenient Passages to them be reserved for the use of the Schollars for the time being and not to be Lett to any Person or Persons whatsoever.

[1] By the 'two towers' are meant the two Southern turrets of the S.W. Tower. On these Bradshaw built two wooden chambers connected by a wooden bridge. They are figured in David King's drawing of the South Aspect of the Abbey Church in Dugdale's *Monasticon* (first edition), vol. I, facing p. 58 (A.D. 1655). But in Hollar's drawing of the W. front, facing p. 60, these turrets are shewn a stage lower than the others, as they were before Bradshaw's building was made.

Eodem Die.

That the Roomes hereafter mencioned vizt: The Parlour a Chamber goeing to it three Chambers above the Parlour a Studdy the Tower Chamber a Gallery two Roomes above the Kitchen a Buttery a Cellar a Cole Howse and Wood Howse the Private Gardine betwixt the Cloysters and the Howse with convenient Passages to them Part of the late Deanes Stable unlett and the Coachhowse nowe in the Possession of the Lord President be Lett unto his Lordship for the terme of 40 yeares if he live so Long.

27 March 1650.

Uppon hearing the Report of the Committee appointed to receive what the Lord President should offer concerning the Former order of the Governors about that Part of the late Deanes Howse they are resolved to Lett to his Lordship. It is ordered That the Further consideracion thereof be referred untill the meeting of the Governors on this Day Seavenight.

4° Aprill 1650.

That the Custodie of the Roomes and Gardine formerlie Reserved by the Governors and the use of them at all such tymes as they or any by their Appointment shall not make use of them for the Service of the Colledge or Common Wealth be Graunted unto the Lord President under the Seale of the Governors dureing the Tearme of his Lordships life.

4th April 1650.

That the Parcells of the late Deanes Howse and Stable be Lett unto the Lord President for the terme of 40 yeares if his Lordship and his Lady or either of them shall Live soe Long.

20th July 1650.

That the Lord President shall have the Lodgings which Mr Paye deceased formerlie had and that they be put into his Lordships Lease of the house.

27th October 1649.

Two Generall Clauses Voted to be putt into all Leases to be made by the Governors (vizt).

(1) That the Lessee shall not Alien nor sett the Leased Howses without the Consent of the Governors.

(2) That the Tennants shall both Putt the saide Howses in Repairacions and so keepe them and soe Leave them.

17th July 1652.

That the Buisnesse concerning the howse which the Lord Bradshaw holdeth be taken into Consideracion on this day fortnight.

20th November 1652.

That Sir William Masham Lord President of the Councell of State Mr Blagrave Mr Gourdon Coll Purefoy Mr Millington Mr Lowe and Sir John Hippesley or any two or more of them be appointed a Committee to state the Matter of Fact concerning the house the Lord Bradshawe holdeth as alsoe what rent is fitt to be sett for the said Howse for time Past and to come and to consider of the charges that the said Lord Bradshawe hath bin at in and about the said Howse and report theire opinions thereof to the Governors on this day fortnight.

Eodem Die.

That Mr Browne and such other person or persons as the Committee shall think fitt doe attend them concerning the buisnesse of the howse which the said Lord Bradshawe holdeth.

Ver: Cop: Extr:

per Johannem Squibb.

[On the outside in the same hand: 'Lord Bradshawes Papers.' Bradshaw was Lord President 1649—52.]

19. *Munim....*

Some consideracions fitt to be propounded[1] to the Committee of the Governors appointed to state matters of fact concerning the house which the Lord Bradshawe houldeth:

That part of the house which is intended to be leased to the Lord Bradshawe containes onely a hall or parlor, a gallerie a kitchin a dineing chamber and withdrawing roome adioyning to it, the Tower chamber, some three Lodging chambers a studie, with some other odd roomes not worth the mencioning, all which are exceeding smokie, ly at such a distance as that they have noe dependance one upon another; the quiet of them is perpetually disturbed by the Schollars and otherwise, and thes roomes being put into very good repaire cannott be worth above per annum.

The little house formerly in Mr Payes houlding containes onely 4 little Smoakie roomes, and twoe closets being placed upon the top

[1] A parallel document (now with the Busby papers) is endorsed in Bradshaw's own hand: 'My Paper touching the Deanes House, &c., propounded for consideration.' From it an extract has been quoted on p. 14.

of the Cloysters right over against Col. Humphreyes house. This house of Col. Humphreyes is far larger and more convenient haveing Cellerage &c. which the other wants and is now let at 8^{li} per annum, soe as if his lordship have the like measure that others have it cannott be valued at above 5^{li} yearely.

The stable houlds about 10 horses and 2 coaches and is worth about 10^{li} yearely.

His Lordship hath already disbursed in repaires and building upon the freehold as appeares by the bills	218 : 17 : 10 :
And is to bestowe in necessary repaires to make it tenantable as appeares by the Certificate of Mr Carter and Mr Stephens to whom it was referred by this Committee.	149 : 08 : 07 :
In all	368 : 06 : 05 :

The house and premisses being subject to casualties and repaires cannott for a Lease for 21 yeares or 2 lives be valued to be worth above 7 yeares and a halfes purchase and 300^{li} of the Summe above (and being accounted as payd by way of ffine) will at that rate strike off 40^{li} a yeare of the rent.

If it be objected the roomes built upon the 2 towers were not necessary but built for pleasure.

It will receive this Answere that it was necessary to cover the towers with leade to preserve them and the very leade came to 46^{li} as appeares by the plummers bill, and the other materialls which are left upon the freehould besides workmanship come to at least 40^{li} more and the whole worke came to 140^{li}, soe as there wilbe but 54^{li} to be deducted out of the 68^{li} : 6^{s} : 5^{d} : remaineing above the 300^{li} before mencioned to be accounted as payd by way of ffine.

20. *Munim.* 42,916.

Order (23 Sept. 1654) to draw up the Lease.

Lease of Deanery to John Bradshaw.

This Indenture made the Thirtith daie of September in the Yeare of our Lord One Thowsand Six Hundred Fiftie and Fower. Betweene the Governors of the Schoole and Almes Howses of the City of Westminster in the Countie of Midds of the one part And John Bradshaw seriaunt att Lawe and Cheife Justice of Chester of the other part Witnesseth that the said Governors takeing notice of the great and extraordinary Charges expended and laid out by the said John Bradshawe in and about the Repaires and inlargement of the Capitall Messuage and other the buildings heereafter mentõned amounting as hath beene made to appeare to Seaven Hundred and Sixtie poundes In Consideracōn thereof and of the yearly Rent heereafter in and by theis presents reserved Of theire owne free assents and Consents for themselves and theire Successors Have in pursuance of the power to them given by the Parliament Demised graunted and to ffarme letten And by theis presents doe Demise graunt and to ffarme let unto the said John Bradshawe all that Capitall Messuage or Tenement Commonly Called or Knowne by the name of the Colledge or the late Deanes House of the Collegiate Church of Peters in the Citty of Westminster in the County of Middlesex scituate lying and being on the South-West end of the said Collegiate Church within the said Citty and Libertie and the Roome called the Tower Chamber together with the Roomes lately built upon the Two Towers adioyning to the said Church by the said John Bradshawe And alsoe the Pipes or Qille of head Waters and Watercourses to the said Capitall Messuage or Tenement belonging And alsoe the Stable Coach-howses usually occupied with the said Capitall Messuage or Tenement together with the Hayloft and Roomes over the said Stable and Coach-howses scituate and being in Stable-yard in the said Citty and the Pipe or Quill of Lead Water and Water-course with the said Stable now used occupied and enioyed And alsoe all those buildings and Lodgings upon the South-West Corner of the great Cloysters in Westminster aforesaid and next adioyning to part of the said Demised premisses with the Appurteñnces heeretofore in the tenure or occupatōn of Nicholas Pay Esqr deceased somtime Auditor to the late Deane and Chapter of Westminster aforesaid And alsoe the Garden comonly called the Deanes privie garden adioyning to the Deanes Yard And alsoe all those other buildings and lodgings scituate and being upon the East part of the said Great Cloysters in Westminster aforesaid with theire and every of theire Appurtennces late or heeretofore in the tenure or occupacōn of Colonell John Humphries deceased his Assignee or Assignes And the little Garden lying betweene the great Cloysters and the said Capitall Messuage together alsoe with the respective Waies and passages leading in to the said Collegiate Church and the Great Cloyster And all other waies waters easements profitts com̄odities and emoluments to the said Demised premisses belonging or to or with the same usually occupied or enioyed or accepted reputed taken or knowne as part parcell or member thereof Except and forth of this present demise alwaies reserved the Great Dyning Hall the Kitchen the Cellar under the Hall the Pastry the Larder Pantry the Butlers Chamber and the Cole-howse without the gate now used and occupied for the use of the Schollers And Excepting to the Governors and theire successors att the times of Electōn the free use of Jerusalem Chamber if they shall see Cause And alsoe Except the Chambers lately used by M[r] Byfeild which are sett apart for the use of the Mynisters that preach the morninge Lecture During the time that the same shalbe soe imployed onely and not otherwise And alsoe except the Chamber called the Governors Chamber And the Clossett there with the Gallery leading thereto And alsoe Excepting the use of all that waie or passage leading to and from the s̄d garden gate to the Gallery for the Use of the said Governors and theire Successors and such as shall attend them att such times as they have occasion to use the same for the service of the said Schoole and Almeshowses And alsoe excepting the Porters Lodge To have and to hould the said Capitall Messuage or tenement and all and singular the said Demised premisses with theire and every of theire Appurtenñes (Except before and in manner and forme before Excepted) unto the said John Bradshawe his executors Administrators and Assignes from the nyne and Twentith daie of September last past before the date of theis presents for and during and unto the full end and terme of Fortie Yeares from thence next and ymediatly ensuing fully to bee compleat and ended in as full and ample manner as the late Deane of the said Collegiate Church of Westminster or any of his Predecessors had held occupied or enioyed the same. Yeilding and paying therefore yearly during the said terme unto the said Governors and theire Successors or to the Receivor Generall or Collector of the Revenue belonging to the said Schoole and Almes-howses of Westminster for the time being or theire Deputie or Deputies in that behalfe the sume of Thirtie poundes of good and lawfull money of England to be paid halfe yearly Att or in the now Common Dyning Hall of the Colledge of Westminster att or upon the Five and Twentith daie of March and Nyne and Twentith daie of September yearly by even and equall porcōns. The first payment thereof to Commence and begynn on the Five and Twentith daie of March next ensuing the date of theis presents. And the said Governors for themselves and theire Successors Doe heereby graunt unto the said John Bradshawe the Custody and use of the said Chamber called the Governors Chamber and the Gallery Leading thereunto......att such time or times as the said Governors or theire Successors shall not make use of them for the service of the said Schoole and Almes-howses. To have and to houlde the use and Custodie of the said two last mencōned Roomes to the said John Bradshawe his Executors Administrators and Assignes. For and dureing and unto the full end and term of the aforemencōned terme of Fortie yeares fully to be compleat and ended And the said John Bradshawe doth for himself his Executors, Administrators and Assignes Covenant and Agree to and with the said Governors and theire Successors by theise presents that hee the said John Bradshawe his Executors Administrators and Assignes shall and will att his and theire proper Costs and Charges from tyme to tyme and att all times during the said terme when and as often as neede shall require well and sufficiently repaire, sustaine and amende all the said demised premisses and the same soe well and sufficiently repaired sustained and amended shall and will leave and yeilde upp unto the said Governors and theire Successors att the end of the said terme. And alsoe that it shall and may be lawfull to and for the said Governors and theire Successors and to their Surveyor of the said Schoole and Almeshowses for the time being or any of them into the said demised Premisses and every or any part thereof att all convenient times during the said terme to enter and the same to Survey, and if any default shall happen to be in the repairac̃ons That then upon monic̃on or warning to be given to the said John Bradshawe his Executors, Administrators and Assignes or left in writing att the said demised premisses of the said defects the same shalbe sufficiently repaired, sustained and amended within six monethes next after such monicōn or warning to be given or left in writing as aforesaid And if it shall happen that the said yearly Rent of Thirtie poundes or any part or parcell thereof shalbe behind and unpaid by the space of Twentie daies next after any of the said daies appointed and lymitted for payment therof in which the same ought to be paid as aforesaid being lawfully demaunded Or if the reparacōns of the demised premisses or any part or parcell therof with the Appurtenñces bee not made and done within Six monethes next after such monicōn or warning therof to be given or left in writing as aforesaid That then and from thenceforth it shall and may be lawfull to and for the said Governors and theire Successors into the said demised premisses or any part therof to reenter and the same to repossesse and have againe as in theire former estate This Indenture or anything therin Conteyned to the Contrary therof in any wise Notwithstanding. And the said Governors for themselves and theire Successors Doe by theis presents Covenaunt graunt and agree to and with the said John

Bradshawe his Executors, Administrators and Assignes by theis presents That hee the said John Bradshawe his Executors Administrators and Assigns under and upon the Rent and Covenants aforesaid shall and may dureing the said terme peaceably and quietly have hould use occupie and enioy all the said demised premisses with the Appurtennces for and dureing the said Terme according to the true intent and meaning of theis presents without the lawfull Lett suite trouble disturbance interupcōn or evictōn of them the said Governors and theire Successors or any other Person or Persons clayming by from or under them in any wise. In witnes whereof aswell the Common Seale of the said Governors as the hand and Seale of the said John Bradshawe to theis Indentures interchangably are put the daie and yeare first above written.

Jo: [seal] Bradshawe.

(On the back) Sealed and deliverd in the presence of

Edmond Sqibb Reg^r.
Joseph Hobbes.
Henry Hitchcock.

21. *Munim.* 42,942—43,031.

The Bills of 1653 and 1654 shew that Bradshaw made a new kitchen (in lieu of 'the old kitchen'), a servants' dining room, a 'gentlemen's dining room' (also called 'the new dining room'), and a new staircase (with a gallery, or perhaps loft, above it).

He also fitted out 'the Abbot's Chamber' and the 'withdrawing room' next to it as 'my Lady's' apartments.

Moreover £55 was spent in leads over the cloisters ('the new platforme'). There is also mention of building a brick-wall over the cloister (the northern wall of the building already there, which had been only of lath and plaster).

Several of the other items are of great interest; but from our lack of knowledge they are not always easy to interpret. Thus in no. 19 we seem to get the date at which Litlyngton's tiles in the 'Abbot's Chamber' were covered over with the present wooden flooring. These tiles extend over the whole of the room, but the surface of them is entirely worn away, except in one or two places. They were examined in 1903, and some of the boards were fitted with hinges, so that the best preserved parts might readily be seen. No. 53, however, suggests that there had been some floor laid over the tiles before this time; but perhaps it only means that the work was at first badly done, and had to be done over again.

The various dining rooms are puzzling. As Bradshaw was excluded from the use of the Abbot's Hall, he evidently had to make fresh provision for his 'gentlemen.' If by 'the new dining room' is meant the present one over the kitchen, we get into difficulty with the item for 'covering the new dyning roome with sheete lead': for we should have to suppose that the two storeys now above it were not built by Bradshaw and there seems no evidence for assigning them to a later date. It may be that a more careful collation of the bills and their summaries might shew which room was meant.

The Bills are summarised under date 11 June 1653: they extend to the number of 84.

In this summary the following phrases occur:

No. 8. Tyling over the Starecase £9. 16.
10. Emptying 2 vaults.
11. Emptying a vault.
18. Making a Siellen, Partitions in the buttery.
19. Laying the Joyce and boarding the floare in the Abbott's Chamber.
35. Cutting away for the Starecase and for 2 doores.
36. Taking up the floore in the Chamber over the buttery.
44. Deales to finish the starecase £8. 17. 10 (besides £1. 12 in No. 28).
46. Glasing the new starecase.
48. Plastering the New Starecase, a new chamber over it £26. 11.
50. Making a great starecase, a chamber over it, a little starecase, a House of office &c. £75. 16.
(After 52). Disbursed for 16 Large marble Stones which are laid in the new dyning roome chimney £1. 6.
53. Taking up the floare in the Abbott's chamber and new laying it.
56. Culloring.. the matted roome, painting the great starecase the chimney and chimney peice in the gallery.
57. Building the Kitchen, and lesser starecase, turning the old Kitchen into a dyning roome, &c. £36. 11.
58. New tyling the Kitchen, Starecase, &c. £25. 0. 6.
63. A starecase for the waterhouse, a doore, a partition, &c.
64. Covering the new dyning roome with sheete lead £9. 0. 6.
71. Making a bricke wall over the cloyster £8.
72. Painting...my Lord's new Studdy.
74. Laying a marb[l]e footpace in the drawing roome chimney.
76. A shed in the garden.

Sum Total...£464. 13. 2

The Bills themselves contain many further items of interest, *e.g.*:

No. 20. Abbot's Chamber: making the stairs going up to the lodgings (materials included) £2. 6. 8.

25. A key to two locks for Mr Rowe...locks for the Rume where the Righting is.
35. Cutting way for the staircase, and cutting...two doorways and a window.
45. Lead over Gallery £13: lead for gutters over new Rufcast building £2. 3. 0.
47. Lock and key for me ladyes Closit.
The great stairs and the Gallery[1] over it (42,911 A).
Work in the gallery on top of the stairs (42,993 G).
Altering a dormer.
A doorhead going into the servants dining room.
The little stairs by the two great doors.
The old side of the gallery.
Piecing the great door going up into the great dining room.
Lining a window in the lower room under the stairs.
For 39 steps in going up into the Kitchen and going into the upper dining room.
57. For the great window in the new dining room (43,000, May 1654).
14 steps of stairs going up to Mr Higgeson's lodgings (cf. 42,996).
13 steps going up from Kitchen.
Cutting away the floor and the roof for the Kitchen chimney.
59. One day's work to take down the botres [*i.e.* the buttress of the cloister wall, to make place for the kitchen chimney].
4½ days breaking down two doorways going into the Coalhouse: one day to break down the oving.
4 days for sinking the kitchen (?) (43,005 D).
Sheet lead laid over the new dining room (43,007 B).
67. The room over the kitchin.
68. Two doors going into the dining room.
69. The chamber where the gackwaite [jack-weight] goeth.
71. Building a wall over the cloisters (Bricklayer).
79. Mr Parnel's room [Thos. Parnell pays the bills now].
81. The new pantry...the gentelle mens dining rome.
The brickwork in my ladys colsett (43,030).
For laying the footpace in the gentell men chamber.

22. Chapter Orders under Dean Sprat[2].

Sep. 21, 1683. Ordered, That the Deane shall have 40^{li} allow'd him by the Treasurer for the alteracions intended to bee made in his house if it shall amount to soe much.

Oct. 13, 1683. That a Chimney bee built in the Dean's hall att the Charge of the Colledge[3].

[1] This is shewn in the Atterbury plans described below, p. 77.

[2] Installed Sept. 21, 1683.

[3] *Treasurer's Acc^{ts}*. 1683: To my L^{d} By Like Order for his Expences about the new Roome in the Deanry...xxxiii^{li} vi^{s} viij^{d}.

Ibid. 1684: Paid Charges in Building the Dean a New Studdy by Order of Chapter as p Bills...$\overset{\text{xx}}{\text{iiij}}$^{l}x^{li} xij^{s} vi^{d}.

Paid Charges in Repayres in Severall Places about the Deanry as p Bills...xliij^{li} viij^{s} i^{d}.

May 29, 1702. That the sisterne in the great Cloysters which receives the water running to the Dean and Prebendaryes houses be new made and set up, the Old one being fallen down and much in decay and likewise the sistern in the little Cloysters be amended and made good[1].

Apr. 6, 1706. That nothing be done this year to the Dean's and Prebends Houses but only to keep the Roofes in repair.

May 5, 1707. That the Roofe of the Jerusalem Chamber be made good and firme and that the College Pantry and the Butler's Chimney be repaired as the Treasurer shall direct.

Feb. 16, 1707/8. That the Treasurer do view a Closet that is likely to fall down in the Deans House and take care that it be made good.

Feb. 17, 1708/9. That no Worke exceeding the value of 4 pounds upon the Deanery, or 40 shillings upon any Prebendal House be done without a Chapter Order for the same[2].

Feb. 25, 1708/9. That the Battlements over the Deanery and the Colledge Hall be repaired.

May 25, 1709. That part of the Deanery which adjoins to the Registers House, and the Registers House be repaired with all necessary Reparacions after the cheapest manner.

Feb. 14, 1709/10. That the Treasurer do provide what Gravell is necessary to new lay the Deans Garden after such manner as his Ldp shall approve of.

Feb. 30, 1710/11[3]. That a Vault be made in the Deans Cellar according to his Ldps directions.

23. Chapter Orders under Dean Atterbury[4].

July 17, 1713. That the Deanery be repair'd and made fit for his Ldps Reception and a new Roome built according to his Ldps desire, and that Mr Dickenson lay before the next Chapter an Estimate of the whole Charge.

July 24, 1713. That the Deanery be repair'd and a new Roome built next to the Study there, according to the Estimates this day deliver'd into the Chapter.

1 Compare the earlier Order, June 20, 1663: Ordered that Mr Treasurer doe give the Lord Bpp of Worcester [Dean Earles] Satisfaction for the Cisterne standing in the Deanes Kitchin.

2 Repeated, Apr. 4, 1711, and Feb. 14, 1714/5: a similar order had been made Jan. 16, 1672/3.

3 'Tricesimo die Februarij'!

4 Installed June 16, 1713.

May 28, 1718. That the great Roome near the Library in the Deanery and Staires and Doors leading thereto be fitted up upon the College Account in such manner as my L[d] the Dean shall direct.

Nov. 4, 1718. My L[d] the Dean this day acquainted the Chapter that the work order'd in the Deanery by the Chapter Act of the 28th of last May was likely to arrise to a much greater sum than He expected by the Reason of the many more Decays and Defects found in the Building than the Workmen apprehended, and that therefore He had stopt wainscotting and finishing the great Roome and Closett till He had inform'd the Chapter thereof and had their further Consent to finish the same: Whereupon it was unanimously agreed that the same should be compleated at the College Charge in the manner his Lordship should direct.

24. Atterbury's Plans: *Munim.* Press 28.

Four plans are extant, which were drawn with a view to Dean Atterbury's alterations. Three of them are of the year 1715, and are marked '1st Story,' '2[d] Story,' and '3[d] Story.' The first is in fact the ground floor plan. It shews the main entrance into the house as in the centre of the passage under the gallery: to the right on entering is a lobby out of which rise the great stairs constructed by Bradshaw. A little to the left of the present hall-door, and quite in the corner, is a small door leading to a small flight of stairs, just outside the kitchen door: traces of this staircase can still be seen in the entry from the kitchen to the coal cellar: it sprang from within the little tower which originally had the newel staircase. The present staircase leading up from the kitchen did not then exist.

The '2[d] Story' plan shews the 'High Dining Roome' (the present Ante Room), and the 'Great Dining Room' (the present Dining Room) which Bradshaw had built over his new kitchen. It shews a curious arrangement of the rooms over the West Cloister, which then contained a staircase giving access to the rooms above them: a slip is attached which offers an alternative proposal for this staircase. The newel staircase is shewn, both on this floor and on the next, as cut away to insert wooden stairs: see the Plan on p. 6, which is from the '3[d] Story' plan. The first of the Red Rooms, which was built by Dean Sprat, is marked 'Study': to the north of it is a much smaller room, but a suggestion for its enlargement to its present size is sketched in on the plan. The Jericho Parlour bears the name of 'Organ Roome.'

On the '3[d] Story' the rooms above Jericho are called 'M[r] Arch Deacon's Apartment': Bishop Sprat's son being the Archdeacon of Rochester. The chambers built by Dean Neile are shewn as still intact, and are assigned to 'M[r] Low.'

The fourth plan is dated 1718, and is a mixture of plan and elevation. It shews a 'loft' over the staircase, reached by a flight of eight stairs just outside the present dining room door. This is called in a note on the back of the plan the 'Organ Loft.' The elevation shews the top of the tower which had contained the newel staircase, rising four feet above the leads. The new elevation (attached) clears away both the loft and the upper part of the tower, giving the present arrangement. Portions of plan attached shew the second Red Room as already built, nearly as at present, and offer a modification of the great staircase, which however is not in accordance with what now exists and possibly was never carried out.

These plans are of special interest as shewing the house as Bradshaw left it, the only alteration apparently being the addition of the 'Study' off the gallery, built by Dean Sprat.

25. Chapter Orders under Dean Wilcocks[1].

July 7, 1731. That a Sum not exceeding One hundred pounds be allowed to him for putting the Deanary House in Repair, and fitting it up in such manner as He shall think proper.

Dec. 7, 1731. That the Pales Scaffolding and Sheds be removed from the Quadrangle of the Great Cloyster into a large peice of the Deans Garden which is to be a Store and Work yard the Dean consenting thereto for the greater Convenience and ornam[t] of the College. And that Iron Rails with sharp Spikes be put into all the Windows of the said Cloyster and that the Area thereof be made neat Grass ground.

Oct. 4, 1732. That the two Brick Buildings in the great Cloyster be pulled down and the Materials sold and Iron Barrs put into those Windows as in the rest.

Dec. 18, 1733. That the Screen by the Clock be taken down (the Floor made good) and the Materials thereof be used in Wainscotting the Dining Hall: And that the Chapell now behind the Screen be fitted up for a Vestry[2].

[1] Installed July 2, 1731. [Nothing under Dean Bradford.]

[2] In the Account given to Parliament: '1735. On New Wainscotting and Beautifying the College Hall, New Building the Receiver's Office, Repairing the Registry, Almshouses, &c. £218. 16. 8.'

Feb. 21, 1733/4. That the Ceiling of the Jerusalem Chamber, and passage, with that in the Audit Room, be White Washed.

Dec. 16, 1735. That a Sett of new Chairs be bought for the Organ Room.

Apr. 17, 1736. That the Old brick Wall[1] upon the West Cloyster be made good, and covered with Stucco according to an Estimate this day given in (cf. above, no. 21).

An Estimate of Ripping the Roofs of the Deanary and ten prebendal Houses, being this day laid before the Chapter, amounting to about £400—Agreed That the Sum of One hundred and fifty pounds be laid out in Ripping them in their Order, as far as that Sum will go.

May 19, 1736. That the Roof over the Dining Room at the Deanary be repaired according to the Estimate and Account the Chapter have this day had of it from Mr James upon a View thereof by him made on the third Instant, the Great Timber or main Beams being quite decayed and in a ruinous Condition.

That the Jerusalem Chamber Windows be cleaned and amended and a new wire grate be put before the North window thereof to secure it, the Old one being quite worn out.

Mar. 16, 1737/8. That to prevent the annoyance of Smoak in the Jerusalem Chamber and Organ-room, Tin funnells be put upon those Chimneys.

Mar. 3, 1738/9. The hanging Wall over the Great Cloyster Gate being ruinous, and viewed by Mr James Ordered That the same be taken down and the Battlements adjoyning be secured[2].

Mar. 1, 1739/40. That the Carpenters Work needfull to be done at the Deanary, and at Dr Henricks and Mr Barnards Prebendal Houses, amounting to £44. 1. 9, as by Estimate this day produced, be forthwith done.

April 2, 1743. The Dean having this day acquainted the Chapter with a Design of new fitting up the two best Rooms in the Deanery, namely, the High Dining Room and the Drawing Room: by mending and altering the Wainscott and by putting therein two marble Chimney pieces with Slabbs and Carved work: all to remain to the College, Agreed and,

Ordered That His Lordship be allowed and paid by the Treasurer the Sum of twenty pounds towards carrying the same into Execution.

[1] Built by Bradshaw.

[2] In the Report to Parliament: 'Taking down the decayed pediment over the Cloyster Gate and rebuilding the same.'

Having signified also his Intention of new painting this Summer the greatest part of the inside of the Deanry House at his own Charge: Ordered, That the Whitewashing of the Cielings Passages &c. be done as usual by the College and that the Outside Painting thereof amounting by Estimate to £6. 10. 9 be likewise done by the College.

Oct. 17, 1743. That the Passage from the Deanery to the back-yard being about four yards long and four feet broad, formerly laid with Bricks and now worn out, be new laid with Stone, the Expence whereof is Estimated at £2. 12. 0.

That the Bricklayers and Smiths work in taking two Cross Beams out of the new Marble Chimneys, and turning two Arches of Brick in lieu thereof: and Carpenters work in making new inside Shutters to one of the Study windows; Two Closet Doors in a Chamber, and a Dresser in the Kitchen, and in mending stopping and preparing the Wainscott in various places, for the Painter to work upon, be allowed by the College.

We have, moreover, in the Special Order Book for Repairs of Church (1733 onwards):

Feb. 16, 1740. That the Workmen go on with the building of the S.W. Tower of the Abbey, and the other Works; And that the Hoysting Engine and Fence be removed nearer to the said Tower for opening the way to the W. end of the Church according to the Plan this day laid before us by the Mason: And that proper Accommodation be made for Mr Gell in lieu of what shall be pulled down, and that all things be left, when the Work is done, as they were found....

Apr. 8, 1745. That the Battlements at the N. end of the Jerusalem Chamber and along to Mrs Robinson's House be made good by the Bricklayer, and that he build a wall from the Angle of Mr Gell's Wall to the N.W. Angle of the Jerusalem Chamber.

That the Door under the N. Window of the Jerusalem Chamber be taken away, and filled up by the Mason with Stone like the rest of the Wall.

May 7, 1745. Whereas the Approach to the W. Gate of our Collegiate Church would be much handsomer, and on public Solemnities more commodious, if all the Brick-Walls, as well new as old, standing before the Deans' Gallery[1] were removed and taken down, and the Dean is consenting thereunto, It is ordered that Mr Grant Clerck of the Works do direct our College Bricklayers to take all the said Brick-Walls down, and to erect a new Brick-wall on the Back Side of the

[1] See above, p. 15.

said Gallery, inclosing such part of the Dean's Garden as he shall direct and judge sufficient for holding all the Conveniences contained within the Brick-Walls now ordered to be taken down, and that he remove and fit up again all the said Conveniences in the new place when ready for them.

K.

The Norman Chequer Work.

It may be seen by an examination of the large Plan that the tower over the main entrance to the Cloisters extends some ten feet southwards, beyond the wall of the entrance passage. Between this wall and the outer wall of the tower is a space, 26 ft. long and 3 ft. 9 in. wide. On the ground floor this narrow space contains the scullery of the porter's lodge: on the first storey it forms a long and very narrow bedroom. Both of these rooms have been irregularly enlarged by scooping out recesses in the rubble of the thick walls on either side. On the second storey a more systematic enlargement has taken place, the northern wall having been reduced to a mere partition, a foot wide: the space has been divided by a large chimney-breast, and the western portion has yet another small storey above it.

The wall at the eastern end on the second storey shews a large chequer pattern, about 3 ft. 9 in. wide and 13 ft. high, made out of variously coloured stones and tiles. To the north, this pattern originally was bounded by the thick north wall: but that wall has been sliced away for more than a foot of its width, and the part of the face of the east wall which it once covered is now left bare and rough. To the south, the chequer pattern is bounded by the outside wall of the tower, which cuts off what must have been a further extension of the pattern. The junction of wall and pattern has been carefully made, half-diamonds of firestone being used to complete the pattern, where it had been broken away in the building of the wall.

Above the pattern there is a cornice, surmounted by a band of quatrefoils; and this cornice also, with its quatrefoils, is likewise cut short by the outside wall of the tower. This seems to shew that the pattern, whether originally the decoration of an outside wall or not, was at some period so exposed as to need the protection afforded by a cornice. The cornice and quatrefoils, which may perhaps be early fourteenth century work, extend 1 ft. 10 in. upwards, and the wall above them rises plain for about 2 ft. 10 in. to the ceiling of the room: in this upper part of the wall is a small oblong aperture, now filled up.

The illustration here given, from a photograph kindly made for me by Mr Wallace, shews the upper part of the pattern, and the cornice with the quatrefoils; and also the flat-plastered walls enclosing either side. The lower part of the pattern is better preserved. The only thing at all of the same kind in the abbey is a chequer pattern in the south-west corner of the little cloisters, upon the outside wall of the organist's house; and there the work is undoubtedly of the Norman period.

It is not easy to unravel the history to which these interesting features bear witness. The following occurs to me as a possible interpretation. The pattern was on the west face of the west wall of the refectory. The rest of the wall, running south, disappeared; perhaps about 1390, when the range of offices for the cellarer was built; perhaps a little earlier, when Litlyngton built his tower. The wall to the north was a continuation of the refectory wall: above, it has been reduced to very slender dimensions; and, below, it gradually thins away as it goes westwards (see the large Plan), no doubt for the straightening of the reconstructed cloister entrance of Abbot Litlyngton's time. The pattern may have originally decorated a large chamber west of the refectory; and when the chamber disappeared, and the pattern became exposed, the cornice may have been placed above it as an ornamental protection. At any rate, the cornice must be earlier than Abbot Litlyngton's time; for it is cut short by the wall of his entrance tower. The existence of the wall to the north of the pattern, now almost entirely thinned away, suggests that to the west of the Norman Abbot's Camera (over the *locutorium*) there was some building, forming a continuation of the Camera and providing the means of passing from the newel staircase to the Camera.

L.

Where was the Abbot's Chapel?

Something must be said as to the site of the Abbot's Chapel, though the subject is involved in exceptional obscurity. There is no doubt that the abbot had a private chapel at Westminster, as he had at his houses of Denham, Neyte and elsewhere. There are frequent references to 'my lord's chapel' in the abbot's accounts; and, when another chapel than that at Westminster is intended, this generally seems to be made plain. But where was the chapel situated?

1. The Norman Chequer Work

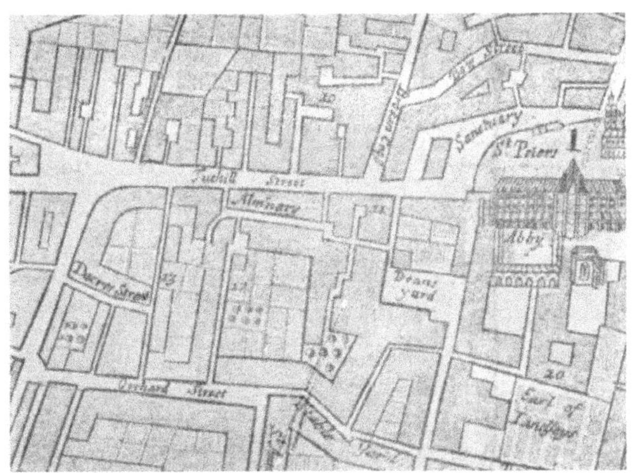

2. From *London, Westminster and Southwark*

By Robt. Morden and Phil. Lea, 1690

10. Swan Inn
11. The King's Alms House
12. The New Way
13. White Hart Lane

It has been commonly said that the easternmost of the two rooms over the cloister entrance, which has beneath the present floor tiles of the fourteenth century, was the Abbot's Chapel. But this room apparently is the *camera abbatis* which was under repair in 1363 (see above in the extracts from Litlyngton's accounts); and it bore the name of the Abbot's Room in 1715. Moreover I think it probable that it is referred to in the Dissolution Inventory, in the note which says: 'Memorandum: the [Deanes] Abbottes Chamber furnysshed complete geven unto hym by the Kynges Commissioners[1].'

We have no direct evidence as to the position of the chapel before Islip's time. Then, however, we find references to a new chapel. Thus in the subsexton's roll for 19 Hen. VIII we have a reference to '½ pound tapers to our fathers new chapel within the monastery and to hys chapel at Hendon[2].' This cannot refer to Islip's Chapel in the north aisle of the presbytery; for that was the Jesus Chapel[3], and it has already been mentioned under 'pound tapers.' Moreover we find in the Dissolution Inventory, among other rooms in the house, 'my lordys newe Chappell,' which is put next after 'Jerico parlor.'

I have little doubt where we must look for it. Islip's new building contained not only Jericho with the rooms below and above it, but also a chamber on the upper floor built in between the S.W. Tower and the first buttress of the Nave, and having a wooden oriel looking into the Church. The tracery of this window is now torn away, and the arch behind it is blocked up with boarding: a partition divides the chamber into a small bedroom and a passage; but this partition is subsequent to 1715. The room as originally constructed, and hung with the tapestries mentioned in the Inventory, may well have served for the Abbot's private mass. It would appear to have retained for some time its sacred character and to be referred to in a later document[4] as the 'Oratorie within Mr Deane Goodmans bedchamber.'

The recurrence in various documents of the expression 'new Chapel' seems to suggest that for some time previously no chapel had been in use: else we should expect the entry for tapers in the accounts to be simply for 'my Lord's Chapel,' whether its position had been changed

[1] The westernmost room, which in 1715 was called the 'Landry,' I should identify with 'the Warderobe at Cheyneygates' mentioned earlier in the same Inventory.

[2] *Munim.* 19,834: cf. 19,828 and 19,836.

[3] I have discussed the problem of the Jesus Chapel at some length in the article 'On the Benedictine Abbey of Westminster,' in the *Church Quarterly Review* for April 1904, pp. 71—75.

[4] See above, p. 63.

or not. Possibly Islip's predecessor, who had let his house at Westminster to Queen Elizabeth Wydville, was not much in residence, and had been contented with an altar specially assigned to him in the Church itself. Thus the old Chapel may have been in a state of decay. Conceivably it occupied part of the site on which Islip's new building rose: that would account for its total disappearance, and would also be in harmony with the general conservatism of monastic building which tended to keep things as much as possible where they were.

A systematic examination of the fifteenth century rolls may possibly throw some further light on the matter.

CAMBRIDGE: PRINTED BY JOHN CLAY, M.A. AT THE UNIVERSITY PRESS